SALESFORCE CERTIFIED PLATFORM DEVELOPER 1

RAPID CERTIFICATION EXAM PREP GUIDE

WITH SAMPLE EXAMS

SALESFORCE CERTIFIED PLATFORM DEVELOPER 1 - RAPID CERTIFICATION EXAM PREP GUIDE

Copyright © 2023 BookWorm Channel

All rights reserved.

ISBN: 9798406573679

DEDICATION

You know how it goes. You pick up a book and flip to the dedication section. You realize that the author has dedicated the book you purchased to someone else but not you.

Not this time.

We might not have met but it does not mean that we will not think fondly of each other…

This book's for you from someone that was in your shoes a couple of years ago, trying to obtain Salesforce certification. Now that I manage to secure that certification, here I am dedicating this book to a knowledge seeker, the future of Salesforce. YOU!

With you know what, and you probably know why.

SALESFORCE CERTIFIED PLATFORM DEVELOPER 1 - RAPID CERTIFICATION EXAM PREP GUIDE

CHAPTER 1 - INTRODUCTION	**1**
CHAPTER 2 - DEVELOPER FUNDAMENTALS	**3**
CHAPTER 3 - PROCESS AUTOMATION AND LOGIC	**12**
CHAPTER 4 - USER INTERFACE	**34**
CHAPTER 5 - TESTING, DEBUGGING AND DEPLOYMENT	**47**
CHAPTER 6 - SAMPLE EXAMS	**56**

ACKNOWLEDGMENTS

Thanks to everyone on my publishing team. Thanks to my wife and my son as well.

They have been very supportive of publishing this book.

It was a tireless effort to deliver this book in a short amount of time so I also want to thank all the Salesforce certified admins taking a look at this book prior to getting released.

CHAPTER 1 - INTRODUCTION

Welcome to the Salesforce Platform Developer I Certification: Rapid Exam Prep, your one-stop guide to successfully prepare for and pass the Salesforce Platform Developer I exam. This book has been carefully designed to provide an in-depth understanding of all the sections and subsections of the certification exam, supplemented with questions and detailed explanations similar to what you'll encounter in the actual exam.

Salesforce has become a global leader in the world of CRM and cloud computing, making Salesforce certifications highly sought after by professionals and organizations alike. The Platform Developer I certification demonstrates your ability to develop custom applications on the Salesforce platform using the Apex programming language, Visualforce, and Lightning Components. Earning this certification will validate your skills and knowledge as a Salesforce developer, opening doors to new career opportunities and helping you stand out among your peers.

SALESFORCE CERTIFIED PLATFORM DEVELOPER I - RAPID CERTIFICATION EXAM PREP GUIDE

This book is organized into chapters that cover the exam sections, with each chapter broken down into subsections that dive deep into the exam topics. The chapters are as follows:

1. Introduction
2. Developer Fundamentals
3. Process Automation and Logic
4. User Interface
5. Testing, Debugging, and Deployment
6. Practice Exams

The first chapter provides an overview of the book's purpose, organization, and approach to helping you prepare for the exam. The subsequent chapters (2-5) cover the key areas of the Platform.

This is a quick prep guide for a reason so grab your favorite drink as quickly as you can and let's dig in!

CHAPTER 2 - DEVELOPER FUNDAMENTALS

In this chapter, we will delve into the Developer Fundamentals section of the Salesforce Platform Developer I certification exam. This section accounts for 23% of the total exam weight and focuses on understanding multi-tenant concepts, design frameworks, declarative versus programmatic customizations, data modeling, and data import/export considerations. By the end of this chapter, you will have a thorough understanding of the core concepts and best practices required for a Salesforce developer in these areas.

2.1 Understanding Multi-Tenant Concepts and Design Frameworks

The Salesforce platform is built on a multi-tenant architecture, which allows multiple customers (also known as tenants) to share the same underlying infrastructure and resources while maintaining the privacy and security of their data. This efficient approach enables Salesforce to provide a scalable, cost-effective, and reliable platform for its customers. As a Salesforce developer, it is crucial to understand multi-tenant concepts and design frameworks like the Model-View-Controller (MVC) architecture and the Lightning Component Framework.

Question:

Universal Containers is planning to build a custom application on the Salesforce platform. They want to ensure that their application adheres to the best practices for multi-tenant architecture. Which of the following design frameworks should they consider implementing in their custom application? (Choose one.)

A. Model-View-Controller (MVC) architecture

B. Monolithic architecture

C. Microservices architecture

D. Serverless architecture

Answer:

A. Model-View-Controller (MVC) architecture

Explanation:

The Model-View-Controller (MVC) architecture is a design framework that separates an application's data (model), user interface (view), and business logic (controller) into distinct components. This separation of concerns promotes modularity, maintainability, and scalability, making it well-suited for building custom applications on the Salesforce multi-tenant platform. The other options, Monolithic, Microservices, and Serverless architectures, are not specifically recommended for Salesforce development and do not take into account the unique considerations of the Salesforce multi-tenant platform.

2.2 Declarative vs. Programmatic Customizations: Use Cases and Best Practices

Salesforce offers two primary approaches for customizing its platform: declarative and programmatic. Declarative customizations involve configuring the platform using built-in tools, such as formula fields, roll-up summary fields, validation rules, and process automation features like Process Builder and Flow. Programmatic customizations involve writing code, such as Apex classes, triggers, Visualforce pages, and Lightning Components. As a Salesforce developer, it is essential to understand when to use each approach, the associated best practices, and the impact of governor limits on your customizations.

Question:

Cloud Kicks, a shoe retailer, wants to create a custom Salesforce application to automate their sales processes. They need to implement a solution to automatically update the status of an opportunity when certain conditions are met. Which of the following approaches should Cloud Kicks consider for this customization? (Choose two.)

A. Create an Apex trigger to update the opportunity status.
B. Use a formula field to update the opportunity status.
C. Implement a Process Builder to update the opportunity status.
D. Write a Visualforce page to update the opportunity status.

Answer:

A. Create an Apex trigger to update the opportunity status.
C. Implement a Process Builder to update the opportunity status.

Explanation:

For this scenario, both an Apex trigger and a Process Builder can be used to update the opportunity status based on specific conditions. An Apex trigger is a programmatic approach that offers more flexibility but requires coding and maintenance. Process Builder is a declarative approach that allows you to configure the update without writing code. The choice between the two options depends on the complexity of the conditions and the organization's preference for declarative or programmatic customizations.

Using a formula field to update the opportunity status is not a suitable option, as formula fields are read-only and used for displaying calculated values. Writing a Visualforce page is also not appropriate for this requirement, as Visualforce pages are primarily used for custom user interfaces rather than automating processes.

2.3 Data Modeling: Objects, Fields, Relationships, and External IDs

Data modeling is the process of defining and organizing data structures within Salesforce to represent real-world entities and their relationships. In Salesforce, objects represent entities (e.g., Accounts, Contacts), while fields represent the attributes of these entities (e.g., Account Name, Contact Email). Relationships between objects can be created using various types of relationships, such as lookup, master-detail, or many-to-many (junction object). External IDs are used to uniquely identify records when integrating with external systems. As a Salesforce developer, understanding how to create and work with objects, fields, relationships, and external IDs is vital to building custom applications.

Question:

Universal Containers is building a custom application to manage its products and related accessories. They require a data model that allows them to associate multiple accessories with multiple products, and each accessory can be related to more than one product. Which of the following data modeling approaches should Universal Containers implement to achieve this requirement? (Choose one.)

A. Create a lookup relationship between the Product and Accessory objects.
B. Create a master-detail relationship between the Product and Accessory objects.
C. Create a junction object to establish a many-to-many relationship between the Product and Accessory objects.
D. Add a multi-select picklist field to the Product object to store related accessories.

Answer:

C. Create a junction object to establish a many-to-many relationship between the Product and Accessory objects.

Explanation:

To create a many-to-many relationship between the Product and Accessory objects, Universal Containers should use a junction object. A junction object is a custom object with two master-detail relationships, one to each of the related objects (in this case, Product and Accessory). This approach allows multiple accessories to be associated with multiple products, and each accessory can be related to more than one product.

Creating a lookup relationship between the Product and Accessory objects would establish a one-to-many relationship, which does not meet the requirement. A master-detail relationship would also create a one-to-many relationship and enforce a parent-child dependency between the objects, which is not suitable for this scenario. Adding a multi-select picklist field to the Product object is not an ideal solution, as it can lead to data integrity issues and does not provide the flexibility and scalability of a junction object.

2.4 Data Import and Export: Options and Considerations

Salesforce provides various tools and options for importing and exporting data into and out of development environments. Data import and export are essential for migrating data between orgs, integrating with external systems, and ensuring data integrity during deployments. As a Salesforce developer, understanding the available tools and best practices for importing and exporting data is crucial for managing data efficiently and securely.

Question:

Cloud Kicks is integrating their Salesforce instance with an external system. They need to import large amounts of data from the external system into Salesforce while ensuring data integrity and minimizing the risk of hitting governor limits. Which of the following tools should Cloud Kicks consider for this data import? (Choose two.)

A. Data Import Wizard
B. Data Loader
C. External Objects
D. Apex Data Loader

Answer:

B. Data Loader
D. Apex Data Loader

Explanation:

For large-scale data imports, Data Loader and Apex Data Loader are suitable options. Data Loader is a standalone tool provided by Salesforce for importing, exporting, and deleting data in Salesforce. It supports CSV files and can handle large data volumes while offering features like batch processing, error handling, and upsert operations. Apex Data Loader is an open-source alternative to Data Loader that uses the Salesforce Bulk API for importing and exporting data, also supporting large data volumes and offering similar features.

The Data Import Wizard is a user-friendly tool built into Salesforce, but it has limitations on the number of records it can process, making it unsuitable for large-scale data imports. External Objects are used to access data stored outside of Salesforce in real-time via OData services, which does not align with the requirement of importing large amounts of data into Salesforce.

—

In Chapter 2, we explored the Developer Fundamentals section of the Salesforce Platform Developer I certification exam. This section covers crucial concepts such as multi-tenant architecture, design frameworks, declarative and programmatic customizations, data modeling, and data import and export options. We examined the importance of understanding and applying best practices for each of these areas, including the use of the Model-View-Controller (MVC) architecture, deciding when to use declarative or programmatic customizations, creating and managing objects, fields, relationships, and external IDs, and choosing the appropriate tools for data import and export. By mastering these fundamentals, you will be better equipped to develop efficient, scalable, and maintainable custom applications on the Salesforce platform.

CHAPTER 3 - PROCESS AUTOMATION AND LOGIC

In this chapter, we will dive into the Process Automation and Logic section of the Salesforce Platform Developer I certification exam. This section accounts for 30% of the exam weight and focuses on the capabilities of declarative process automation features, Apex control flow statements, SOSL, SOQL, DML statements, governor limits, save order of execution, recursion, cascading, and exception handling. By the end of this chapter, you will have a comprehensive understanding of process automation and logic in Salesforce, preparing you to tackle questions related to these topics on the exam.

3.1 Declarative Process Automation Features

Salesforce offers a range of declarative process automation features that enable you to automate business processes without writing code. These features include Workflow Rules, Approval Processes, Process Builder, and Flow. As a Salesforce developer, understanding the capabilities and use cases of these declarative process automation features is essential when designing and implementing custom solutions on the platform.

Question:

Universal Containers wants to automate their sales process by updating the account owner when an opportunity reaches a specific stage. They prefer to use a declarative solution that does not require Apex code. Which of the following declarative process automation features should Universal Containers use to achieve this requirement? (Choose one.)

A. Workflow Rule
B. Approval Process
C. Process Builder
D. Visualforce

Answer:

C. Process Builder

Explanation:

Process Builder is the most suitable declarative process automation feature for this scenario. It allows you to create a process with a specific criteria, such as the opportunity to reach a certain stage, and perform an action like updating a related record, in this case, the account owner. Process Builder provides a visual interface for designing and configuring processes without writing Apex code.

Workflow Rules can perform field updates but cannot update related records, such as the account owner in this case. Approval Processes are used for defining multi-step approval processes and do not serve the purpose of updating related records based on specific criteria. Visualforce is a framework for creating custom user interfaces, not for automating business processes.

3.2 Apex: Variables, Constants, Methods, Modifiers, and Interfaces

Apex is Salesforce's proprietary programming language, designed to facilitate the creation of custom business logic on the platform. In Apex, you can define variables, constants, methods, modifiers, and interfaces to build reusable, modular, and scalable code. Understanding the syntax, structure, and use cases of these elements is essential for Salesforce developers when implementing custom solutions.

Question:

Cloud Kicks is developing a custom application to manage its inventory. They need to create a class with a method that calculates the total inventory value based on the price and quantity of each product. Which of the following Apex code snippets correctly implements this requirement? (Choose one.)

A.
```apex
public class InventoryManager {
    public Integer calculateTotalInventoryValue(Decimal price, Integer quantity) {
        return price * quantity;
    }
}
```

B.
```apex
public class InventoryManager {
    public Decimal calculateTotalInventoryValue(Decimal price, Integer quantity) {
        return price * quantity;
    }
}
```

C.
```apex
public class InventoryManager {
    private Decimal calculateTotalInventoryValue(Decimal price, Integer quantity) {
        return price * quantity;
    }
}
```

D.
```apex
public interface InventoryManager {
    Decimal calculateTotalInventoryValue(Decimal price, Integer quantity);
}
```

Answer:

B.
```
public class InventoryManager {
    public Decimal calculateTotalInventoryValue(Decimal price, Integer quantity) {
        return price * quantity;
    }
}
```

Explanation:

Option B is the correct implementation of the requirement. It defines a public class called InventoryManager and a public method called calculateTotalInventoryValue that accepts two parameters, price and quantity, and returns the result of their multiplication as a Decimal value.

Option A uses the wrong return type (Integer) for the calculateTotalInventoryValue method, as the product of price and quantity could result in a Decimal value. Option C uses a private modifier for the calculateTotalInventoryValue method, making it inaccessible outside the InventoryManager class, which may not align with the intended use case. Option D defines an interface instead of a class, which does not provide an implementation of the calculateTotalInventoryValue method as required.

3.3 Apex Control Flow Statements

Control flow statements in Apex enable developers to control the execution of code based on specific conditions or iterations. These statements include loops (for, while, and do-while), conditionals (if, if-else, and switch), and exception handling (try, catch, and finally). Mastering the use of control flow statements allows you to create efficient, modular, and dynamic Apex code to address various business requirements.

SALESFORCE CERTIFIED PLATFORM DEVELOPER I - RAPID CERTIFICATION EXAM PREP GUIDE

Question:

Universal Containers has a list of opportunity records and wants to update the opportunity names to include the stage name if the stage is 'Closed Won.' Which of the following Apex code snippets correctly implements this requirement? (Choose one.)

A.
```
List<Opportunity> oppList = [SELECT Id, Name, StageName FROM Opportunity];
for(Opportunity opp : oppList) {
   if(opp.StageName == 'Closed Won') {
      opp.Name = opp.Name + ' - ' + opp.StageName;
   }
}
update oppList;
```

B.
```
List<Opportunity> oppList = [SELECT Id, Name, StageName FROM Opportunity];
for(Integer i = 0; i < oppList.size(); i++) {
   if(oppList[i].StageName != 'Closed Won') {
      continue;
   }
   oppList[i].Name = oppList[i].Name + ' - ' + oppList[i].StageName;
}
update oppList;
```

C.
```
List<Opportunity> oppList = [SELECT Id, Name, StageName FROM Opportunity];
for(Opportunity opp : oppList) {
   if(opp.StageName != 'Closed Won') {
      break;
   }
   opp.Name = opp.Name + ' - ' + opp.StageName;
}
update oppList;
```

D.
```
List<Opportunity> oppList = [SELECT Id, Name, StageName FROM Opportunity WHERE StageName = 'Closed Won'];
for(Opportunity opp : oppList) {
   opp.Name = opp.Name + ' - ' + opp.StageName;
}
update oppList;
```

Answer:

D.
```
List<Opportunity> oppList = [SELECT Id, Name, StageName FROM Opportunity WHERE StageName = 'Closed Won'];
for(Opportunity opp : oppList) {
    opp.Name = opp.Name + ' - ' + opp.StageName;
}
update oppList;
```

Explanation:

Option D is the correct implementation of the requirement. It queries opportunities with the 'Closed Won' stage using a SOQL query with a WHERE clause and then iterates through the retrieved records using a for loop, updating the opportunity names as required. The code efficiently filters the records during the query, reducing the number of iterations and processing only the relevant opportunities.

Option A and B both use an if statement to check if the stage is 'Closed Won,' which is less efficient than filtering the records at the query level. Option C uses a break statement, which would terminate the loop as soon as it encounters an opportunity that does not meet the condition, potentially leaving other relevant opportunities unprocessed.

3.4 Writing SOSL, SOQL, and DML Statements in Apex

Salesforce Object Search Language (SOSL) and Salesforce Object Query Language (SOQL) are powerful languages used to search and query data in Salesforce. DML (Data Manipulation Language) statements allow you to create, update, delete, and restore data records. In Apex, you can write SOSL, SOQL, and DML statements to interact with the Salesforce database, retrieve, and manipulate data. As a Salesforce developer, it's essential to understand how to use these statements effectively and adhere to best practices.

Question:

Cloud Kicks wants to find all contacts with the last name 'Smith' and update their mailing city to 'San Francisco.' Which of the following Apex code snippets correctly implements this requirement? (Choose one.)

A.
```
List<Contact> contacts = [SELECT Id, MailingCity FROM Contact WHERE LastName = 'Smith'];
for(Contact c : contacts) {
   c.MailingCity = 'San Francisco';
}
update contacts;
```

B.
```
List<Contact> contacts = [FIND 'Smith' IN ALL FIELDS RETURNING Contact (Id, MailingCity)][0];
for(Contact c : contacts) {
   c.MailingCity = 'San Francisco';
}
update contacts;
```

C.
```
Contact[] contacts = [SELECT Id, MailingCity FROM Contact WHERE LastName = 'Smith'];
for(Contact c : contacts) {
   c.MailingCity = 'San Francisco';
}
Database.update(contacts);
```

D.
```
Contact[] contacts = [SELECT Id, MailingCity FROM Contact WHERE LastName = 'Smith'];
for(Contact c : contacts) {
   c.MailingCity = 'San Francisco';
}
Database.update(contacts, false);
```

Answer:

A.
List<Contact> contacts = [SELECT Id, MailingCity FROM Contact WHERE LastName = 'Smith'];
for(Contact c : contacts) {
   c.MailingCity = 'San Francisco';
}
update contacts;

Explanation:

Option A is the correct implementation of the requirement. It uses a SOQL query to retrieve contacts with the last name 'Smith,' iterates through the records using a for loop, updates the mailing city, and then uses a DML update statement to save the changes.

Option B uses a SOSL query, which is not the most efficient way to search for records based on a specific field value. SOQL is more suitable for this scenario. Options C and D use Database.update(), which can be used for updating records, but in this scenario, a simple update statement (as in option A) is more straightforward and sufficient. Option D also uses the optional second parameter (false) in the Database.update() method, which allows partial success during the update operation, but it is unnecessary in this context.

3.5 Writing Apex Classes and Triggers

Apex classes and triggers are the building blocks of custom functionality in Salesforce. Classes are containers for Apex code that define methods, variables, and other elements, while triggers execute automatically when specific events occur on Salesforce records. Understanding how to write efficient and modular Apex classes and triggers, following best practices, and adhering to governor limits is crucial for Salesforce developers when implementing custom solutions.

Question:

Cloud Kicks wants to automatically update an account's custom field 'Total_Revenue__c' to the sum of all its associated closed won opportunity amounts. Which of the following Apex trigger code snippets correctly implements this requirement? (Choose one.)

A.
```
trigger UpdateTotalRevenue on Opportunity (after insert, after update) {
   Set<Id> accountIds = new Set<Id>();

   for(Opportunity opp : Trigger.new) {
     if(opp.StageName == 'Closed Won') {
       accountIds.add(opp.AccountId);
     }
   }

   CloudKicksHelper.updateTotalRevenue(accountIds);
}
```

B.
```
trigger UpdateTotalRevenue on Opportunity (before insert, before update) {
   Set<Id> accountIds = new Set<Id>();

   for(Opportunity opp : Trigger.new) {
     if(opp.StageName == 'Closed Won') {
       accountIds.add(opp.AccountId);
     }
   }

   CloudKicksHelper.updateTotalRevenue(accountIds);
}
```

C.
```
trigger UpdateTotalRevenue on Account (after update) {
   Set<Id> accountIds = new Set<Id>();

   for(Opportunity opp : Trigger.new) {
     if(opp.StageName == 'Closed Won') {
       accountIds.add(opp.AccountId);
     }
   }

   CloudKicksHelper.updateTotalRevenue(accountIds);
}
```

D.
```
trigger UpdateTotalRevenue on Opportunity (after insert, after update) {
   List<Account> accountsToUpdate = new List<Account>();

   for(Opportunity opp : Trigger.new) {
     if(opp.StageName == 'Closed Won') {
       accountsToUpdate.add(new Account(Id = opp.AccountId, Total_Revenue__c = opp.Amount));
     }
   }

   update accountsToUpdate;
}
```

Answer:

A.

java
Copy code
```
trigger UpdateTotalRevenue on Opportunity (after insert, after update) {
   Set<Id> accountIds = new Set<Id>();

   for(Opportunity opp : Trigger.new) {
      if(opp.StageName == 'Closed Won') {
         accountIds.add(opp.AccountId);
      }
   }

   CloudKicksHelper.updateTotalRevenue(accountIds);
}
```

Explanation:

Option A is the correct implementation of the requirement. It creates an after insert and after update trigger on the Opportunity object, iterates through the records in Trigger.new, checks if the stage is 'Closed Won,' and adds the AccountId to a set. The trigger then calls the CloudKicksHelper.updateTotalRevenue method, passing the set of account IDs. This approach follows best practices by delegating the processing logic to a helper class.

Option B uses a before insert and before update trigger, which is not the correct event for this requirement, as it would not have access to the final record values. Option C creates a trigger on the Account object, which is not appropriate, as the trigger should be on the Opportunity object. Option D updates the Total_Revenue__c field directly within the trigger, which is not a best practice, as it could lead to potential issues like recursion and does not properly separate the logic into a helper class.

3.6 Governor Limits and Apex Transactions

Governor limits are Salesforce's way of ensuring that resources are shared efficiently across the multi-tenant environment. Apex code is subject to various limits, such as the number of SOQL queries, DML statements, and CPU time. Understanding these limits and how to write efficient Apex code that avoids hitting them is essential for Salesforce developers. Additionally, it's crucial to understand how Apex transactions work and their implications on governor limits.

Question:

Universal Containers has implemented an Apex trigger that updates Account records. They are experiencing occasional errors due to exceeding governor limits. Which of the following best practices could help avoid hitting governor limits in this scenario? (Choose two.)

A. Use SOQL queries within loops to ensure each record is processed correctly.
B. Perform DML operations on collections of records rather than individual records.
C. Utilize helper classes to separate the trigger logic and processing.
D. Use Apex classes instead of triggers for processing records.
E. Implement @future methods to process records asynchronously.

Answer: B, C

Explanation:

B. Performing DML operations on collections of records rather than individual records is a best practice to minimize the number of DML statements, thus reducing the chances of hitting governor limits.

C. Utilizing helper classes to separate the trigger logic and processing promotes modular and efficient code that can help manage governor limits more effectively.

Option A is incorrect because using SOQL queries within loops can quickly lead to exceeding the governor limit on the number of SOQL queries. Option D is incorrect because Apex classes alone cannot replace triggers for processing records in response to specific DML events. Option E is incorrect because, while @future methods can be used to process records asynchronously, they are not directly related to managing governor limits in a trigger scenario and have their own set of limits. Using asynchronous Apex when it is not required can also introduce unnecessary complexity.

3.7 Save Order of Execution and Recursion

Understanding the save order of execution is essential for Salesforce developers to ensure that their custom logic behaves as expected. When a record is saved, a series of events take place, including the execution of validation rules, workflows, and triggers. Knowing the order in which these events occur can help developers avoid unexpected behaviors and potential issues. Additionally, it's important to understand the concept of recursion, which can occur when a trigger or process updates a record, causing the same trigger or process to fire again, leading to potential governor limit issues or infinite loops.

Question:

Universal Containers has a trigger on the Account object that updates related Contacts. This trigger is causing an unintended recursion, and they need to prevent it. Which of the following approaches can help avoid recursion in this scenario? (Choose two.)

A. Use a static variable to control the trigger execution.
B. Use a before update trigger instead of an after update trigger.
C. Move the logic to an Apex class and call the class from the trigger.
D. Implement a validation rule to prevent updates that would cause recursion.
E. Use the System.runAs() method to execute the trigger as a different user.

Answer: A, C

Explanation:

A. Using a static variable to control the trigger execution is a common technique to prevent recursion. The variable can be set to true or false to control whether the trigger should execute its logic, preventing it from running multiple times in the same transaction.

C. Moving the logic to an Apex class and calling the class from the trigger allows for better separation of concerns and can help avoid recursion by encapsulating the logic and allowing for better control over the execution flow.

Option B is incorrect because using a before update trigger instead of an after update trigger does not inherently prevent recursion. Option D is incorrect because validation rules are used to enforce data integrity, not to control trigger execution or prevent recursion. Option E is incorrect because the System.runAs() method is used in test classes to run test methods with different user contexts and does not help prevent recursion in triggers.

3.8 Exception Handling and Custom Exceptions

Exception handling is a fundamental aspect of Apex development, as it allows developers to manage errors and unexpected situations gracefully. It is essential to understand how to use try-catch-finally blocks to handle exceptions and provide appropriate error messages or fallback actions. In addition to standard exceptions, Salesforce developers can create custom exceptions to handle application-specific error conditions.

Question:

Cloud Kicks has implemented an Apex trigger that performs complex calculations on Opportunity records. Occasionally, the trigger encounters errors due to invalid data, and they want to provide more specific error messages to users. Which of the following best practices should they follow when implementing exception handling in their trigger? (Choose two.)

A. Use a try-catch-finally block to handle standard exceptions and custom exceptions.
B. Use System.assert() to provide detailed error messages for users.
C. Create custom exception classes to handle application-specific error conditions.
D. Use a single catch block to handle all exception types in the trigger.
E. Catch DmlException and add error messages to the appropriate record.

Answer: A, C

Explanation:

A. Using a try-catch-finally block in the trigger allows developers to handle both standard exceptions and custom exceptions, ensuring that errors are caught and appropriate actions are taken.

C. Creating custom exception classes helps handle application-specific error conditions by defining custom exceptions with appropriate error messages, making it easier for users to understand and resolve the issue.

Option B is incorrect because System.assert() is used in test classes to validate expected outcomes, not to provide error messages for users. Option D is incorrect because using a single catch block for all exception types can lead to less specific error messages and make it more difficult to handle different error scenarios. Option E is incorrect because, although catching DmlException and adding error messages to the appropriate record is a valid approach for handling DML errors, it does not directly address the requirement of providing more specific error messages for the custom calculations performed in the trigger.

3.9 Combining Declarative and Apex Solutions

Salesforce provides a powerful mix of declarative and programmatic tools for automating business processes. Declarative tools like Process Builder, Workflow Rules, and Flows can often address many common business needs without writing any code. However, more complex requirements may necessitate the use of Apex. Combining declarative and Apex solutions enables developers to build highly customized, efficient, and maintainable applications.

Question:

Universal Containers has a requirement to send an email notification to the Account owner when an Opportunity reaches the "Closed Won" stage. They also need to apply a custom discount calculation on the Opportunity based on the Account's industry. Which of the following approaches should be used to implement this requirement? (Choose two.)

A. Use a Process Builder to send the email notification when the Opportunity stage changes to "Closed Won."
B. Use an Apex trigger to send the email notification and apply the custom discount calculation.
C. Use a Workflow Rule to send the email notification when the Opportunity stage changes to "Closed Won."
D. Use an Apex trigger to apply the custom discount calculation and a Process Builder to send the email notification.
E. Use a Flow to apply the custom discount calculation and send the email notification.

Answer: A, D

Explanation:

A. Using a Process Builder to send the email notification when the Opportunity stage changes to "Closed Won" is a declarative solution that does not require code and is easy to maintain.

D. Using an Apex trigger to apply the custom discount calculation ensures that complex logic can be handled effectively. Combining this with a Process Builder to send the email notification allows for a mix of declarative and programmatic solutions to address the different requirements efficiently.

Option B is incorrect because, while an Apex trigger could be used to send the email notification and apply the custom discount calculation, it is not the most efficient solution, as the email notification requirement can be addressed using a declarative tool. Option C is incorrect because Workflow Rules are less flexible and powerful than Process Builder, making Process Builder a better choice for sending the email notification. Option E is incorrect because, although a Flow can handle complex logic, using an Apex trigger for the custom discount calculation is likely to provide better performance and maintainability.

CHAPTER 4 - USER INTERFACE

4.1 Visualforce Pages and Controllers

Subsection Overview:

Visualforce is a powerful, tag-based markup language that allows developers to create custom user interfaces and interactions within Salesforce. Visualforce pages can be used to display, create, or modify Salesforce data, and can be supported by standard or custom controllers or controller extensions, which provide the necessary logic and data access. Understanding the capabilities of Visualforce and the relationship between pages, controllers, and extensions is essential for Salesforce Platform Developers.

Question:

Universal Containers wants to create a custom Visualforce page to display a list of Contacts related to an Account. They need the ability to filter the list by a specific contact role. Which of the following approaches should be used to implement this requirement? (Choose two.)

A. Use a standard controller for the Account object and a custom controller extension to implement the filtering logic.
B. Use a custom controller to query the Contacts related to the Account and implement the filtering logic.
C. Use a standard controller for the Contact object to display the related Contacts without any filtering options.
D. Utilize a standard list controller to display the related Contacts and implement the filtering logic.
E. Use a standard set controller for the Contact object to display the related Contacts with built-in filtering options.

Answer: A, B

Explanation:

A. Using a standard controller for the Account object and a custom controller extension to implement the filtering logic provides a balance between leveraging built-in functionality and adding custom behavior. The standard controller manages the Account object, while the custom extension handles the filtering logic.

B. Using a custom controller to query the Contacts related to the Account and implement the filtering logic provides full control over the data retrieval and filtering process, allowing developers to create a tailored solution for the requirement.

Option C is incorrect because, while a standard controller for the Contact object can display related Contacts, it does not provide filtering options. Option D is incorrect because standard list controllers are used for displaying lists of records of a specific object, not related records with custom filtering logic. Option E is incorrect because standard set controllers are used for displaying lists of records with built-in pagination and filtering options, but they do not provide a way to display related Contacts or apply custom filtering logic.

4.2 Lightning Component Framework and Content Types

The Lightning Component Framework is a powerful and modern UI framework for creating custom user interfaces and interactions in Salesforce. It is essential for Salesforce Platform Developers to understand the framework, its benefits, and the types of content that can be contained in a Lightning Web Component (LWC). With LWCs, developers can create reusable components that provide better performance, modularity, and maintainability compared to Visualforce or Aura components.

Question:

Cloud Kicks wants to create a custom user interface to display and manage product inventory. They need a fast, modern, and responsive solution that can be used on both desktop and mobile devices. Which of the following approaches should they use to implement this requirement? (Choose two.)

A. Create a Lightning Web Component (LWC) to build the custom user interface with better performance and modularity.
B. Use a Visualforce page with a custom controller to build the custom user interface.
C. Utilize Aura components to build the custom user interface with built-in responsiveness.
D. Create a custom mobile app using Salesforce Mobile SDK and use LWCs for the user interface.
E. Embed an external application built with a modern web framework, like React or Angular, within a Visualforce page.

Answer: A, D

Explanation:

A. Creating a Lightning Web Component (LWC) to build the custom user interface provides a modern, fast, and responsive solution. LWCs are built using standard web technologies and offer better performance and modularity compared to Visualforce or Aura components.

D. Creating a custom mobile app using the Salesforce Mobile SDK and using LWCs for the user interface combines the power of the Salesforce platform with the flexibility and performance of LWCs. This approach provides a tailored mobile experience while maintaining a consistent look and feel across devices.

Option B is incorrect because, while a Visualforce page can be used to build custom user interfaces, it does not provide the same level of performance, responsiveness, or modularity as LWCs. Option C is incorrect because, although Aura components can provide a responsive user interface, they do not offer the same level of performance and modularity as LWCs. Option E is incorrect because embedding an external application within a Visualforce page can add complexity, increase maintenance efforts, and may not provide the same level of integration with Salesforce as LWCs or Aura components.

4.3 User Interface and Data Access Security

Ensuring the security of user interfaces and data access is a top priority for any Salesforce Platform Developer. It is essential to understand the various security features and best practices available within the platform to prevent vulnerabilities and protect sensitive information. Developers must consider how to implement secure access controls, prevent cross-site scripting (XSS) attacks, enforce CRUD and FLS permissions, and utilize sharing settings in their custom user interface components.

Question:

Universal Containers wants to ensure that their custom Lightning Web Component (LWC) adheres to best practices for user interface and data access security. Which of the following actions should they take to achieve this goal? (Choose two.)

A. Use the with sharing keyword in Apex classes to enforce record-level access control.
B. Use the without sharing keyword in Apex classes to ensure that all users can access necessary data.
C. Utilize the lightning-input component to mitigate cross-site scripting (XSS) attacks.
D. Bypass CRUD and FLS checks in Apex classes to optimize performance.
E. Ensure that the LWC enforces CRUD and FLS permissions when displaying or modifying records.

Answer: A, C

Explanation:

A. Using the with sharing keyword in Apex classes enforces record-level access control, ensuring that users can only access records they have permission to view or modify. This helps maintain the security of data access in custom components.

C. Utilizing the lightning-input component in LWCs provides built-in protection against cross-site scripting (XSS) attacks. The lightning-input component automatically sanitizes user input and prevents malicious scripts from being executed.

Option B is incorrect because using the without sharing keyword would allow Apex classes to bypass record-level access control, which could result in unauthorized data access. Option D is incorrect because bypassing CRUD and FLS checks in Apex classes may lead to data access vulnerabilities and compromise the security of the user interface. Option E is correct in principle, but it is not a specific action to take; rather, it is a best practice to follow when developing custom components.

4.4 Custom User Interface Components

Salesforce Platform Developers can create custom user interface components to enhance the overall user experience and better meet the unique needs of an organization. These components can include Lightning Components, Flow, Visualforce, and more. Understanding the use cases and best practices for implementing these components in various scenarios is crucial for a developer's success.

Question:

Cloud Kicks wants to create a custom user interface to streamline the order management process, allowing their sales team to manage opportunities and related order records more efficiently. They want to make use of Salesforce's native features as much as possible. Which of the following approaches should they use to implement this requirement? (Choose two.)

A. Create a custom Lightning Web Component (LWC) that displays a list of opportunities and their related order records in a unified view.
B. Implement a Flow to guide users through the order management process, embedding it on the opportunity record page.
C. Use a Visualforce page with a custom controller to display opportunities and related order records.
D. Implement a Next Best Action strategy to guide users through the order management process.
E. Create a custom object tab to display order records related to opportunities.

Answer: A, B

Explanation:

A. Creating a custom Lightning Web Component (LWC) allows Cloud Kicks to build a modern, responsive, and efficient user interface that displays a list of opportunities and their related order records in a unified view. This approach enables the sales team to manage opportunities and orders more efficiently.

B. Implementing a Flow to guide users through the order management process provides a step-by-step, interactive experience. By embedding the Flow on the opportunity record page, users can quickly and easily complete tasks related to order management without leaving the context of the opportunity.

Option C is incorrect because, while a Visualforce page can be used to create custom user interfaces, it does not provide the same level of performance, responsiveness, or modularity as LWCs. Option D is incorrect because Next Best Action strategies are typically used for providing guidance on recommended actions based on specific criteria, rather than streamlining a process like order management. Option E is incorrect because creating a custom object tab would display all order records, not just those related to specific opportunities, which does not meet the requirement to streamline the order management process.

4.5 Lightning Web Component Events

In the Lightning Web Component (LWC) framework, events play an essential role in enabling components to communicate with each other and respond to user interactions. Developers must understand the use cases and best practices for LWC events, including how to create and handle custom events, and the difference between component events and application events.

Question:

Universal Containers is building a custom LWC that allows users to search for and select products from their catalog. They want to ensure that when a product is selected, related components on the page are updated accordingly. Which of the following approaches should they use to achieve this requirement?

A. Implement a component event to notify related components when a product is selected.
B. Implement an application event to notify related components when a product is selected.
C. Use Apex to query the database and update related components when a product is selected.
D. Utilize a Visualforce page to handle communication between components.

Answer: A

Explanation:

A. Implementing a component event enables the custom LWC to communicate with related components when a product is selected. Component events propagate up the component hierarchy, allowing parent components to listen for and handle the event, updating their state accordingly.

Option B is incorrect because application events are not supported in the LWC framework. Instead, component events and the pubsub module are recommended for component communication. Option C is incorrect because using Apex to query the database and update related components would introduce unnecessary complexity and could negatively impact performance. Option D is incorrect because utilizing a Visualforce page is not the recommended approach for handling communication between LWCs, as it does not provide the same level of performance, responsiveness, or modularity as LWC events.

4.6 Integrating Apex with Page Components

Subsection Overview:

Salesforce Platform Developers often need to integrate Apex with various types of page components, including Lightning Components, Flow, Next Best Actions, and more. Understanding how to effectively use Apex in combination with these components is crucial for creating custom solutions that meet the unique needs of an organization and enhance the overall user experience.

Question:

Cloud Kicks wants to create a custom LWC that displays a list of top-selling products based on sales data from the past quarter. The LWC should update in real-time as new sales are recorded. Which of the following approaches should they use to implement this requirement? (Choose two.)

A. Create an Apex class with the @AuraEnabled annotation to query top-selling products based on sales data.
B. Use a Visualforce page with a custom controller to query and display top-selling products.
C. Implement a Flow to query top-selling products and embed it on a Lightning record page.
D. Utilize the @wire decorator in the LWC to call the Apex method and retrieve the top-selling products.
E. Use a Next Best Action strategy to display top-selling products based on sales data.

Answer: A, D

Explanation:

A. Creating an Apex class with the @AuraEnabled annotation allows the custom LWC to call the Apex method and retrieve the top-selling products based on sales data. This enables the LWC to display up-to-date sales information.

D. Utilizing the @wire decorator in the LWC to call the Apex method ensures that the component retrieves the top-selling products and updates in real-time as new sales are recorded. The @wire decorator allows developers to declaratively bind data returned by the Apex method to properties in the LWC, automatically refreshing the component when the data changes.

Option B is incorrect because a Visualforce page does not provide the same level of performance, responsiveness, or modularity as a Lightning Web Component. Option C is incorrect because a Flow is not designed to display real-time data updates in the way that the requirement specifies. Option E is incorrect because Next Best Action strategies are typically used for providing guidance on recommended actions based on specific criteria, rather than displaying real-time sales data.

CHAPTER 5 - TESTING, DEBUGGING AND DEPLOYMENT

5.1 Writing and Executing Tests

Subsection Overview:

Writing and executing tests for triggers, controllers, classes, flows, and processes is an essential part of the Salesforce development process. Proper test coverage ensures the stability, reliability, and maintainability of the codebase. Developers must be familiar with various sources of test data and know how to create test classes and methods to validate the functionality of their customizations.

Question:

Universal Containers has recently implemented a custom Apex trigger to enforce a business rule: whenever an opportunity is marked as Closed Won, a follow-up task should be created for the opportunity owner. As a developer, you need to write a test class for this trigger. Which of the following steps should you take to ensure proper test coverage? (Choose two.)

A. Use test setup methods to insert test data for opportunities and tasks.
B. Call the Test.startTest() method before executing the trigger in the test context.
C. Use the System.runAs() method to test the trigger as different users with various profiles.
D. Execute anonymous Apex to directly call the trigger during the test.
E. Query for the task created by the trigger and use System.assertEquals() to validate the expected outcome.

Answer: A, E

Explanation:

A. Using test setup methods to insert test data for opportunities and tasks ensures that you have a consistent set of data to use in your test methods. This approach also helps to minimize code duplication and improve test performance.

E. Querying for the task created by the trigger and using System.assertEquals() to validate the expected outcome is crucial for verifying that the trigger is functioning correctly. This step helps you to confirm that the trigger creates the follow-up task as expected when the opportunity is marked as Closed Won.

Option B is incorrect because the Test.startTest() method is typically used to reset governor limits before executing the code being tested, which is not relevant to this specific scenario. Option C is incorrect because the System.runAs() method is not necessary for this test case, as the trigger logic does not depend on different users or profiles. Option D is incorrect because executing anonymous Apex is not the recommended way to test triggers; instead, you should create a test method that inserts or updates records, causing the trigger to fire automatically.

5.2 Salesforce Developer Tools

Salesforce provides a suite of developer tools, such as Salesforce DX, Salesforce CLI, and Developer Console, that enable developers to streamline their development process, automate tasks, and troubleshoot issues. Understanding when and how to use these tools effectively is crucial for developers working on the Salesforce platform.

Question:

Cloud Kicks is working on a new project that requires the development of several custom Lightning components, Apex classes, and triggers. They want to ensure that their development team follows best practices and has access to the appropriate tools for version control, continuous integration, and streamlined deployments. Which of the following Salesforce Developer tools should they use to meet these requirements? (Choose two.)

A. Salesforce DX
B. Developer Console
C. Salesforce CLI
D. Workbench
E. Data Loader

Answer: A, C

Explanation:

A. Salesforce DX is a set of tools and features that enable developers to build, test, and deploy Salesforce applications in a modern, source-driven development environment. By using Salesforce DX, Cloud Kicks can manage version control, automate deployments, and streamline their development process.

C. Salesforce CLI is a command-line interface that works in conjunction with Salesforce DX, allowing developers to perform various tasks, such as creating scratch orgs, deploying metadata, and running tests. The Salesforce CLI helps developers automate repetitive tasks and integrate their Salesforce development process with external tools and services.

Option B is incorrect because the Developer Console is primarily a lightweight, browser-based development environment suitable for quick edits and debugging but lacks the features necessary for version control, continuous integration, and streamlined deployments. Option D is incorrect because Workbench is a web-based suite of tools designed for administrators and developers to interact with Salesforce organizations, but it does not provide the same level of development support as Salesforce DX and Salesforce CLI. Option E is incorrect because Data Loader is a tool for importing and exporting data in Salesforce, not for managing the development process.

5.3 Debugging System Issues and Monitoring Processes

Subsection Overview:

Debugging system issues and monitoring processes, flows, asynchronous and batch jobs are crucial tasks for Salesforce developers. Understanding how to approach troubleshooting and monitoring these elements ensures that customizations function correctly and efficiently, and helps maintain the overall health of the Salesforce environment.

Question:

Universal Containers has implemented an Apex Batch class to process a large volume of records. Users have reported that the batch job is not processing records as expected. As a developer, which of the following steps should you take to troubleshoot and resolve the issue? (Choose two.)

A. Use the Developer Console to check the debug logs for the batch job execution.
B. Modify the batch job to send an email with detailed error information to the developer.
C. Use the System.schedule() method to run the batch job at a different time.
D. Check the Apex Jobs page in Setup to review the job status and any error messages.
E. Monitor the batch job in real-time using the Workbench REST API.

Answer: A, D

Explanation:

A. Using the Developer Console to check the debug logs for the batch job execution allows you to review the execution details, identify any errors or issues, and gain insights into the root cause of the problem. Debug logs contain valuable information on the execution context, including governor limit usage, errors, and other relevant data.

D. Checking the Apex Jobs page in Setup provides an overview of the job status and any error messages related to the batch job execution. This information can help you identify issues and understand the cause of any processing failures.

Option B is incorrect because, while sending an email with detailed error information can be helpful, it is not the most efficient way to troubleshoot issues with batch jobs. It's better to use the Developer Console or the Apex Jobs page to review error messages and debug logs directly. Option C is incorrect because changing the schedule of the batch job does not address the root cause of the issue. Option E is incorrect because monitoring the batch job in real-time using the Workbench REST API is not a practical method for troubleshooting batch job issues; using the Developer Console or Apex Jobs page is more effective.

5.4 Deployment Environments, Requirements, and Processes

Subsection Overview:

Understanding deployment environments, requirements, and processes is essential for Salesforce developers. Deployments involve moving code and associated configurations from one Salesforce environment to another, often from a sandbox to a production org. Developers need to be familiar with the best practices, tools, and methods for deploying changes in a controlled and efficient manner.

Question:

Cloud Kicks is about to deploy a set of customizations from their sandbox environment to their production org. These customizations include new Apex classes, triggers, and Lightning components. Which of the following best practices should they follow to ensure a successful deployment? (Choose two.)

A. Deploy all changes in a single deployment package to minimize the risk of errors.
B. Use a version control system to track changes and manage deployments.
C. Deploy changes directly from the Developer Console to avoid using additional tools.
D. Validate the deployment package in the target environment before deploying.
E. Deploy changes during business hours to ensure immediate user feedback.

Answer: B, D

Explanation:

B. Using a version control system to track changes and manage deployments helps maintain a clear history of customizations, streamlines the deployment process, and enables the development team to collaborate more effectively. Version control systems, such as Git, are essential for following best practices in Salesforce development.

D. Validating the deployment package in the target environment before deploying helps identify and address any issues or errors that may occur during the deployment process. This step ensures that any potential conflicts or dependencies are resolved before the changes are applied to the production org.

Option A is incorrect because deploying all changes in a single deployment package can increase the risk of errors and make it more challenging to troubleshoot issues. It's better to break changes into smaller, manageable packages when possible. Option C is incorrect because deploying changes directly from the Developer Console is not a recommended best practice; instead, developers should use tools like Salesforce DX, Salesforce CLI, or Change Sets for deployments. Option E is incorrect because deploying changes during business hours can disrupt users and lead to unexpected issues; it's better to schedule deployments during periods of low system usage, such as outside business hours or during maintenance windows.

CHAPTER 6 - SAMPLE EXAMS

Now that you have a fairly good understanding of each section and question style, it is time to test your skills on sample exams!

For any questions you might have, please feel free to contact us at burak@bookwormchannel.com.

SAMPLE EXAM I (60 questions, 105 minutes)

Question 1:
A developer is required to override the standard Opportunity view button using a Visualforce page. What should the developer do?
Choose 1 answer.

A. Use the StandardListController
B. Use a controller extension
C. Use the Opportunity StandardController
D. Use a custom controller and replicate the opportunity detail page

Question 2:
What will be the result if the code below is executed when the variable testRawScore is 75?
Choose 1 answer.

```
if (testRawScore >= 90) {
   gradeEqual = 'Grade A';
} else if (testRawScore >= 80) {
   gradeEqual = 'Grade B';
} else if (testRawScore >= 70) {
   gradeEqual = 'Grade C';
} else if (testRawScore >= 60) {
   gradeEqual = 'Grade D';
}
System.debug(gradeEqual);
```

A. Grade B
B. Grade C
C. Grade A
D. Grade D

Question 3:
A developer is required to create a customized page that displays data from a web service callout. Which of the following options could the developer use for this requirement?
Choose 2 answers.

A. Custom Controller
B. Standard Controller and Extension
C. Standard Controller
D. Standard List Controller

Question 4:
The IT Director of Cosmic Service Solutions is concerned about Cross-Site Scripting (XSS) attacks. Which of the following functions can be used by developers to neutralize potential XSS threats?
Choose 3 answers.

A. JSINHTMLENCODE()
B. JSENCODE()
C. HTMLENCODEINJS()
D. HTML(JSENCODE())
E. HTMLENCODE()

Question 5:
What steps are required to create test data from files using static resources?
Choose 2 answers.

A. Call System.loadData within the test method
B. Call Test.loadData within the test method.
C. Create a static resource and edit to add test data
D. Create the test data in a .csv file and upload to create a static resource

Question 6:
A developer needs to execute an automated process when a platform event outside the Salesforce database occurs. How might this be configured?
Choose 3 answers.

A. Subscribe a flow in Flow Builder to wait for incoming platform event messages.
B. Set up email notifications to notify the admin when an external event occurs.
C. Use the Salesforce REST API to submit a platform event from another system.
D. Use Process Builder to set up a process to manage an incoming platform event.
E. Set up a workflow rule that will notify the admin when an external event occurs.

Question 7:
What type of relationship is appropriate when an external object is acting as a parent to a standard or custom child object and records are matched by an external ID?
Choose 1 answer.

A. Indirect Lookup
B. Parent External Lookup
C. Lookup relationship
D. External Lookup

Question 8:
An administrator is trying to send emails to certain users from a sandbox using a workflow email alert but has found that emails are not being received. What action should be taken?
Choose 3 answers.

A. Check the System Logs
B. Check the Workflow Logs
C. Check the Email Logs
D. Check the email addresses
E. Check email deliverability settings

Question 9:
A company would like to send record information to a legacy system when a criterion is met. Which of the following options can a developer use to accomplish this requirement?
Choose 1 answer.

A. Process Builder
B. Outbound Notification Rule
C. Outbound Message
D. Assignment Rule

Question 10:
What is true regarding working on Salesforce projects using Visual Studio Code?
Choose 2 answers.

A. Code is developed locally and Apex tests can be initialized from Visual Studio Code
B. Each developer can define their own set of metadata files to include in a local project
C. Code in an authorized org depending on the edition can be edited remotely from the editor
D. Each developer will always have the same set of metadata files in their project directory

Question 11:
Which environment would be the most appropriate to perform a test deployment and final regression testing, as well as stress and performance testing?
Choose 1 answer.

A. Development
B. Production Support
C. Staging
D. Quality Assurance

Question 12:
A record-triggered flow uses an invocable Apex method that performs a validation process over multiple related records when the value of the 'Status__c' field on the triggering record is changed. An update needs to be made to invoke different invocable methods, depending on the old and new values of the 'Status__c' field. How should this requirement be handled?
Choose 1 answer.

A. Use the Assignment element in Flow Builder to enable the flow to access the old and new values of the field that triggered the flow.
B. Configure the record-triggered flow to access and compare the old and new values of the field and conditionally invoke methods.
C. Replace Flow Builder with Process Builder since processes can access old and new values of a record using the PRIORVALUE() function.
D. Replace the record-triggered flow with an Apex trigger that compares the old and new values of the field using the Trigger context variables.

Question 13:
A developer is exploring the capabilities of Tooling API while working on the development of an app. Which of the following are the typical use cases of Tooling API?
Choose 3 answers.

A. Committing changes to a Salesforce org
B. Deploying setup configurations into a production org using an XML file
C. Creating the definition of a custom object
D. Accessing code coverage test results for an Apex class
E. Using ApexLog to access a debug log

Question 14:
When a trigger fires, it can process multiple records so all triggers should be written to accommodate bulk transactions. Which of the following are typical examples of bulk transactions?
Choose 3 answers.

A. Data import
B. Bulk Force.com API calls
C. Lightning Events
D. Mass actions
E. Visualforce Actions

Question 15:
A company has a requirement to track the vehicles assigned to work orders. Vehicles can exist without Work Orders and have a record owner. What kind of relationship should be created between Work Orders and Vehicles?
Choose 1 answer.

A. Hierarchy
B. Picklist
C. Lookup
D. Master-Detail

Question 16:
Given the interface and class below. What is the expected result if the class is instantiated?
Choose 1 answer.

```
/** interface **/
public interface document {
   String getTitle(String prefix);
}
/** class **/
public class diploma implements document {
   public String title = 'New Document';
   public String getTitle(String newPrefix) {
      return newPrefix + ' ' + title;
   }
   public void setDate() {
      /* do something */
   }
   public diploma() {
      if (String.isBlank(title)) {
         System.debug('No Title');
      } else {
         System.debug(title);
      }
   }
}
```
A. "New Document" will be printed in the log.
B. "No Title" will be printed in the log.
C. Code will not even compile because the parameter name of the getTitle method does not match with the interface.
D. Code will not even compile because of the extra method setDate which is not defined in the interface.

Question 17:
What will be the output if the code below is executed when the value of testRawScore variable is 75?
Choose 1 answer.

```
if (testRawScore >= 90) {
   gradeEqual = 'A';
}
if (testRawScore >= 80) {
   gradeEqual = 'B';
}
if (testRawScore >= 70) {
   gradeEqual = 'C';
}
if (testRawScore >= 60) {
   gradeEqual = 'D';
}
System.debug('Value of gradeEqual = ' + gradeEqual);
```

Question 18:
Which of the following best describe the Lightning Component framework?
Choose 2 answers.

A. It has an event-driven architecture
B. It is device-aware and supports cross-browser compatibility
C. It automatically upgrades all pre-existing Visualforce pages and components
D. It requires the Aura Components model to build Lightning components

Question 19:
A developer notices that the code below returns only 20 Account records though she expected 60. Which of the following is true regarding SOSL query limits?
Choose 1 answer.

FIND {test} RETURNING Account(id), Contact, Opportunity LIMIT 60
A. Limits cannot be set in SOSL queries
B. Results were evenly distributed among the objects returned.
C. Limits have to be individually assigned per object.
D. The SOSL Syntax is incorrect.

Question 20:
How would a developer write a query to return the number of leads for each lead source?
Choose 1 answer.

A. SELECT COUNT(LeadSource) FROM Lead
B. SELECT GROUP(LeadSource) FROM Lead
C. SELECT LeadSource, COUNT(Name) FROM Lead GROUP BY LeadSource
D. SELECT COUNT(*) FROM Lead GROUP BY LeadSource

Question 21:
Of the following, which can use a roll-up summary field?
Choose 3 answers.

A. Accounts using the values of related opportunities
B. Opportunities using the values of opportunity products related to the opportunity
C. Contact using the values of related cases
D. Campaigns using the values of campaign member custom fields
E. Account using the values of related cases

Question 22:
Which of the following actions can be performed in the Before Update trigger?
Choose 2 answers.

A. Delete trigger.new values to avoid changes.
B. Modifying trigger.old values.
C. Change its own field values using trigger.new.
D. Create a validation before accepting own field changes.

Question 23:
A developer has created two custom objects with API names \'Sales Order__c\' and \'Shipment__c\' to track orders and shipments related to them. Sales Order is the parent in the master-detail relationship between the two objects. The Shipment object has a custom field named \'Tracking_Number__c\' that indicates the tracking number associated with a particular shipment. The developer is writing an Apex class in which he needs to retrieve all the sales orders and the tracking numbers associated with their shipment records using a SOQL query. Which of the following represents the correct syntax of the query?
Choose 1 answer.

A. SELECT Name, (SELECT Tracking_Number__c FROM Sales_Order__c.Shipment__c) FROM Sales_Order__c
B. SELECT Name, (SELECT Tracking_Number__c FROM Shipments__r) FROM Sales_Order__c
C. SELECT Sales_Order__c.Name, Shipment__c.Tracking_Number__c FROM Sales_Order__c, Shipment__c
D. SELECT Name, (SELECT Tracking_Number__c FROM Shipment__c) FROM Sales_Order__c

Question 24:
A Salesforce developer has written the code block below that performs certain logic based on the type of field returned. The developer notices that when more values need to be compared, the block becomes harder to read and more code is being duplicated. Which is a suitable option to make the code more readable and at the same time reduce its size?
Choose 1 answer.

Schema.DisplayType fieldType = fieldName.getDescribe().getType();
if (fieldType == DisplayType.String || fieldType == DisplayType.EncryptedString || fieldType == DisplayType.TextArea ||
    fieldType == DisplayType.Combobox || fieldType == DisplayType.MultiPicklist || fieldType == DisplayType.Picklist) {
    // handle as string value
} else if (fieldType == DisplayType.Integer || fieldType == DisplayType.Double || fieldType == DisplayType.Long ||
    fieldType == DisplayType.Percent || fieldType == DisplayType.Currency) {
    // handle as numeric value
} else if (fieldType == DisplayType.Date || fieldType == DisplayType.DateTime || fieldType == DisplayType.Time) {
    // handle as date/time value
} else if (fieldType == DisplayType.Boolean) {
    // handle as boolean value
} else {
    // handle as something else
}

A. Use a switch block with multiple values
B. Create nested if-else statements
C. Use a switch block with single values
D. Split block into separate if statements

Question 25:
In an effort to securely display data in an organization, a developer is modifying any existing custom controllers that do not use a sharing declaration. Which of the following can be used in the definition of a custom controller class to ensure that only records for which the running user has sharing access are displayed when a Visualforce page invokes the class?
Choose 2 answers.

A. The 'with sharing' keywords
B. The 'sharing' access modifier
C. The 'protected' access modifier
D. The 'inherited sharing' keywords

Question 26:
The developers of Cosmic Enterprises use sandbox environments for development, integration, and testing. A developer often needs to migrate metadata components from one sandbox to another when multiple developers are working on the same project. The lead developer of the organization would like to simplify the customization of individual sandboxes and reduce the amount of time spent by developers on migrating metadata components. Which option is available for this use case?
Choose 2 answers.

A. An AppExchange application can be used to copy an existing sandbox and create one with the same metadata components.
B. A change set can be created to move metadata components from one sandbox to another.
C. While creating a sandbox, an option to use an existing sandbox can be selected.
D. A sandbox can be cloned to ensure that the same metadata components are available for other developers.

Question 27:
A developer at Cosmic Solutions is creating a Visualforce page that will be added to an Account page layout. The developer needs to iterate through the list of child Contacts for the Account the user is looking at. How can the developer access the list of child Contacts for the current Account in the Visualforce markup?
Choose 1 answer.

A. {! account.contacts }
B. for (Contact c: this.contacts)
C. <apex:repeat value="{! Contacts }" var="myContact">
D. {! contacts }

Question 28:
Which are true about executing an anonymous block of Apex?
Choose 2 answers.

A. Anonymous blocks can include user-defined methods
B. If the APEX code completes successfully, data changes are automatically committed
C. Anonymous blocks can only be compiled and executed using the Developer Console
D. Anonymous blocks always run in the system context

Question 29:
The system administrator of Cosmic Solutions is building a flow that should be triggered after an account record is updated. When the rating of an Account record changes to 'Hot', the flow should automatically send an email to the account manager and send related data to an enterprise resource planning system using Apex code. When the rating changes to 'Cold', it should only send an email to the account manager. Without using the 'Is Changed' operator, which of the following represents the correct way of configuring the outcomes in the Decision element of the flow for this use case? Choose 1 answer.

A. Each outcome should include a condition that checks a custom field that stores the previous value of the 'Rating' field.
B. Each outcome should be configured to check if the value of the $CHANGED global variable is true.
C. Each outcome in the element should be configured to execute 'only if the record that triggered the flow to run is updated to meet the condition requirements'.
D. Each outcome in the element should be configured to execute 'if the condition requirements are met'.

Question 30:
Which of the following statements about defining an Apex Class are true?
Choose 3 answers.

A. The keyword [class] is required if no access modifier is present.
B. An access modifier is required in the declaration of a top-level class
C. A developer may add optional extensions and/or implementations.
D. A definition modifier is required in the top-level class.
E. The keyword [class] followed by the name of the class is necessary

Question 31:
Given the code of a Visualforce page below, what should be the name of the getter method in the associated custom controller?
Choose 1 answer.

```
<apex:page controller="SampleController">
  <apex:pageBlock>
    <apex:pageBlockTable value="{!productList}" var="product">
      <apex:column value="{!product.Name}" />
      <apex:column value="{!product.Cost__c}" />
      <apex:column value="{!product.Description}" />
    </apex:pageBlockTable>
  </apex:pageBlock>
</apex:page>
```
A. setProductList
B. getProductList
C. productListExtension
D. productList

Question 32:
Support agents of Cosmic Service Solutions use a custom console app in Lightning Experience to manage multiple records on a single screen. A developer has created a Visualforce page that allows users to input data related to cases. Which of the following actions are supported for overriding with the Visualforce code in the console app?
Choose 2 answers.

A. Edit
B. Delete
C. Custom Action
D. View

Question 33:
Stock Symbol is a custom field on the Account object. What is the best way to make this field appear on the Contact detail page layout?
Choose 1 answer.

A. Formula Field
B. Roll-Up Summary field
C. Lookup field
D. Requires Apex Code

Question 34:
Which of the following is required when defining an Apex class method?
Choose 1 answer.

A. Access modifiers
B. Input parameters
C. Return type
D. Definition modifiers

Question 35:
Which of the options below represents a valid method declaration in Apex?
Choose 1 answer.

A. static Boolean public method(String param) { ... }
B. public static Boolean method(String param) { ... }
C. public Boolean static method(String param) { ... }
D. Boolean static public method(String param) { ... }

Question 36:
A developer is creating a method in a Visualforce controller class that accepts a String and a List of sObjects as input parameters. How will the data be passed to the method?
Choose 1 answer.

A. The String will be passed by reference and the List will be passed by value.
B. Both parameters will be passed by value.
C. Both parameters will be passed by reference.
D. The String will be passed by value and the List will be passed by reference.

Question 37:
What are valid use cases for using a custom controller in a Visualforce page?
Choose 2 answers.

A. A Visualforce page needs to have new actions beyond the standard controller that it is using.
B. A Visualforce page's functionality needs to run in system mode.
C. The functionality of the standard controller of the Visualforce page needs to be replaced.
D. The save action of the standard controller of the Visualforce page needs to be overridden.

Question 38:
Universal Containers has triggers that fire on updates for accounts, contacts, and opportunities. Each of these triggers contains DML actions that execute before or after a record update. Each of the objects has active approval processes. Which of the following should a developer consider when modifying any of the triggers?
Choose 2 answers.

A. Every trigger will have its own set of DML limits when invoked within a single transaction
B. Every DML statement executed in any of the 3 triggers will count toward the overall limit within a single transaction
C. DML statements should be run inside loops so the Apex compiler can bundle them together for execution
D. Calls to Approval.process() will count toward the DML limit

Question 39:
Which of the files below can the $ContentAsset global value provider reference?
Choose 3 answers.

A. CSS files
B. images
C. JavaScript files
D. font files
E. HTML files

Question 40:
Eric was told that Visualforce is part of the MVC paradigm. In this context, what does MVC stand for?
Choose 1 answer.

A. Master Class Variable
B. Master Control Variable
C. Model Variable Controller
D. Model View Controller

Question 41:

A developer has declared and initialized a variable named 's' of type String[] to store multiple sObject types. He uses the code below to get describe metadata information for the sObject types.

Schema.DescribeSobjectResult[] r = Schema.describeSObjects(s);

Which method of the DescribeSObjectResult class can be used to determine whether an sObject appears as 'Account' in the user interface?
Choose 1 answer.

A. getName()
B. getLabel()
C. isLabel()
D. isName()

Question 42:

Which of the following are valid Apex variables?
Choose 3 answers.

A. Map<ID, String> sampleMap;
B. Boolean y;
C. Currency abc;
D. String a,b,c;
E. Number x;

Question 43:

A custom Lightning application that uses Apex triggers was developed to help project managers supervise tasks and team members. Although the application is working properly for the rest of the users, one of the project managers reported that errors were encountered when performing a certain action in the application. Which of the options below should be used for debugging the issue?
Choose 1 answer.

A. Create an Apex Trigger trace flag.
B. Create a User trace flag.
C. Create a Debug Session trace flag.
D. Create an Apex Class trace flag.

Question 44:
What is true regarding the user interface for different relationship types?
Choose 2 answers.

A. When a lookup relationship to object B is defined on object A, data from object B can appear as a related list on page layouts of object A
B. When a many-to-many relationship is defined between objects A and B using a junction object, data from the junction object can appear in a related list on the page layouts of objects A and B
C. When a master-detail relationship is defined, data from the master or detail object can appear as a custom related list on page layouts of the other object
D. When a lookup relationship to (parent) object B is defined on (child) object A, data from object A can appear as a related list on page layouts of object B

Question 45:
The developer of Cosmic Solutions has created a nightly Apex job that fetches account records from an external portal used by the company. This Apex job involves retrieving account records in batches of 20 per transaction and is scheduled to run every night at 9 pm. A batch class with a method that executes a web service callout has been defined inside a scheduled class. How can the developer determine if the jobs have been running without any issue?
Choose 2 answers.

A. View information about all the completed Apex jobs by navigating to 'Apex Jobs' in Setup.
B. View information about all the completed Apex jobs by navigating to 'Jobs' in Setup.
C. View information about all the future jobs that are scheduled to run by navigating to 'Scheduled Jobs' in Setup.
D. View information about all the future jobs that are scheduled to run by navigating to 'Apex Flex Queue' in Setup.

Question 46:
Cosmic Supermarket uses a custom object called 'Warehouse' to store information in Salesforce about the company's warehouses. A custom Lightning record page has been created to allow users to view and edit warehouse information. Each warehouse record contains information about multiple warehouse managers and their email addresses. Each warehouse manager is assigned to one or more categories of products. Users who can access a warehouse record should be able to send an email to warehouse managers by specifying one or more product categories. In order to meet this requirement, a Salesforce Administrator is creating a screen flow that can be launched using a quick action on the Lightning page. Which of the following should be considered to ensure that the flow gets the required information from the warehouse record to send the email?
Choose 1 answer.

A. An Apex action is required in the flow to access the warehouse record.
B. The Lightning page needs to be edited to enable passing the warehouse record to the flow.
C. An element needs to be added to the flow to get the warehouse record.
D. The flow should use a record variable named 'recordId' that is available for input.

Question 47:
Which are true regarding a StandardSetController?
Choose 3 answers.

A. It can be used to allow 'list controllers' similar to pre-built Visualforce list controllers to be created.
B. The maximum record limit for StandardSetController is 1,000 records.
C. It can be used to allow 'pre-built list controllers' to be extended
D. The maximum record limit for StandardSetController is 50,000 records.
E. It can be used for mass updates.

Question 48:
Global Insurance would like users to be able to enter policy and advisor details on a screen. When a user clicks the 'Next' button on the screen, the advisor commission related to the details entered by the user should be displayed on the next screen. What would be the recommended solution for this requirement?
Choose 1 answer.

A. Create a Visualforce wizard
B. Create a flow with Flow Builder
C. Create an approval workflow
D. Create a process with Process Builder

Question 49:
An Apex trigger is subscribed to a platform event and generates invoice records upon receiving published event messages from an external order management system. However, an issue has been found on the record creation, and the Apex trigger needs to be modified. It is required that no published event messages should be lost while the Apex trigger is being fixed. What should be done to fix the Apex trigger?
Choose 1 answer.

A. Schedule receiving of platform event messages at a later date or time.
B. Deactivate the Apex trigger and pause publishing of event messages.
C. Suspend the subscription of the Apex trigger to the platform event.
D. Store any published event messages in a custom object temporarily.

Question 50:
Which resource in the Lightning component bundle contains the custom icon resource for components used in the Lightning App Builder or Experience Builder?
Choose 1 answer.

A. CSS Styles
B. Design
C. SVG File
D. Helper

Question 51:
Which of the following are capabilities of schema builder?
Choose 3 answers.

A. Creating a custom object
B. Deleting a custom object
C. Creating lookup and master-detail relationships
D. Exporting schema definition
E. Importing schema definitions

Question 52:
The developer of Bright Starts Company is designing a Lightning web component to mimic the look and feel of the company website on a Lightning page. Which of the following correctly describes the files bundled in this component's folder?
Choose 3 answers.

A. The XML configuration file fetches data from the company website
B. The CSS file is used to style the component and match the company's branding guidelines
C. The JavaScript file defines how the component UI reacts to client events
D. The HTML file defines the UI structure of the component
E. The test file is included to test component functionality and is executed inside Salesforce

Question 53:
Which of the following types of trace flags can be used by a developer?
Choose 3 answers.

A. Class-based
B. Query-based
C. JavaScript-based
D. Trigger-based
E. User-based

Question 54:
A construction company in the housing development business uses the Contact object to track different types of contacts they deal with on a daily basis. The company's Salesforce developer is building a feature for its partner contacts and has written the code below to determine information about a specific record type. Which line of code should be added to line 5?
Choose 1 answer.

1. RecordType recType = [SELECT Id,Name FROM RecordType
2.   WHERE SobjectType='Contact' AND DeveloperName='PartnerContact'
3.   LIMIT 1];
4. Schema.DescribeSObjectResult result = Schema.SObjectType.Contact;
5.
6. Schema.RecordTypeInfo recordTypeInfo = mapRecTypes.get(recType.id);

A.
Map<Id,Schema.RecordTypeInfo> mapRecTypes = result.getRecordTypeInfosById();
B.
Map<Id,Schema.RecordTypeInfo> mapRecTypes = result.getRecordTypeInfos();
C.
Map<Id,Schema.RecordTypeInfo> mapRecTypes = result.getRecordTypes();
D.
Map<Id,Schema.RecordTypeInfo> mapRecTypes = result.getRecordTypeIds();

Question 55:
Which of the following Apex control statements allows a developer to iterate on each element of a collection of an unknown size?
Choose 1 answer.

A. For(Type variable: listOrSet) loop
B. Do-While loop
C. While loop
D. While-Do loop

Question 56:
A Salesforce developer is building a Lightning Aura component and is refactoring code to create a common function that will be reused by several other JavaScript functions in the component. Which file in the component bundle should contain the common function?
Choose 1 answer.

A. The helper file
B. The controller file
C. The component file
D. The design file

Question 57:
Where can a developer use Visualforce in Lightning Experience?
Choose 3 answers.

A. Chatter Feed
B. Standard Page Layout
C. Navigation Bar
D. Custom App
E. Setup Home Page

Question 58:
Which iteration components can be used to display a table of data in a Visualforce page?
Choose 2 answers.

A. <apex:outputTable>
B. <apex:table>
C. <apex:dataTable>
D. <apex:pageBlockTable>

Question 59:
There is a requirement to validate that the country code of an account field is a valid ISO code. There are over 200 codes. What could be used for this validation?
Choose 1 answer.

A. Validation Rule
B. After Update trigger
C. Workflow Rule
D. Before Update trigger

Question 60:
What will happen when the following code is executed?
Choose 2 answers.

```
trigger CaseTrigger on Case (after insert) {
    List<Case> casesToInsert = new List<Case>();
    for (Case parent: Trigger.new) {
        Case child = new Case();
        child.ParentId = parent.Id;
        child.Subject = parent.Subject + ' Child';
        casesToInsert.add(child);
    }
    insert casesToInsert;
}
```

A. No parent or child cases will be created.
B. Child cases will be inserted for each Parent case.
C. The trigger will throw an exception because it is not bulkified.
D. The trigger will be recursively called and result in an infinite loop.

SAMPLE EXAM I ANSWER KEY

Question 1 Answer:
C. Use the Opportunity StandardController

When overriding buttons with a Visualforce page, the standard controller for the object on which the button appears must be used. For example, if one wants to use a page to override the View button on Opportunity, the page markup must include the standardController="Opportunity" attribute on the <apex:page> tag. A controller extension can also be used when one needs to add extra functionality to the Visualforce page that they are using as an override.

Question 2 Answer:
B. Grade C

Repeated ELSE-IF statements will navigate down through each IF and ELSE IF statement UNTIL ONE of the expressions evaluates to true. Even though the last else-if statement contains a condition that is true, it is not executed. The code stops after evaluating the prior statement and assigning the value 'Grade C' to the variable 'gradeEqual'.

Question 3 Answer:
A. Custom Controller
B. Standard Controller and Extension

A custom controller can be used for displaying data from a web service callout, as this action is not supported in standard controllers by default. Alternatively, an extension class can be used to extend the functionality of a standard controller to allow it to perform such action. Similar to a standard controller, a standard list controller is not capable of performing custom actions and is ideal for displaying a list of records.

Question 4 Answer:
A. JSINHTMLENCODE()
B. JSENCODE()
E. HTMLENCODE()

The following functions can be used to neutralize potential XSS threats:

1) HTMLENCODE() – This function allows performing additional HTML encoding of input prior to reflection in HTML context.
2) JSENCODE() – This function can be used to perform JavaScript encoding of input prior to reflection in JavaScript context.
3) JSINHTMLENCODE() – Before the introduction of auto-HTML encoding, developers called this function when including merge-fields in JavaScript event handlers within HTML.
4) JSENCODE(HTMLENCODE()) – This function can be used in place of JSINHTMLENCODE().

Question 5 Answer:
B. Call Test.loadData within the test method.
D. Create the test data in a .csv file and upload to create a static resource

The steps in utilizing the Test.loadData method would be as follows: Add the data in a .csv file, then create a static resource for this file. Next, call Test.loadData within the test method passing to it the sObject type token and the static resource name.

Question 6 Answer:
A. Subscribe a flow in Flow Builder to wait for incoming platform event messages.
C. Use the Salesforce REST API to submit a platform event from another system.
D. Use Process Builder to set up a process to manage an incoming platform event.

Developers can automate business processes that are triggered by events that happen outside the Salesforce database. Using platform events and the REST API, an external system (a networked printer, for example) can call out to the Salesforce org. That call is received and can be handled by a process created in Process Builder. The call can also be handled by a flow that is subscribed to wait for that platform event using either a platform event-triggered flow or a Pause element in Flow Builder. Workflow is used to automate standard internal processes and procedures.

Question 7 Answer:
D. External Lookup

An external lookup relationship links a child standard, custom, or external object to a parent external object.
A lookup relationship is used to link a child standard or custom object to a parent standard or custom object.
An indirect relationship is used to link a child external record to a parent standard or custom object. There is no "Parent External Lookup" relationship type in Salesforce. This concept describes the "External Lookup" relationship.

Question 8 Answer:
C. Check the Email Logs
D. Check the email addresses
E. Check email deliverability settings

The email deliverability setting can prevent emails from getting sent if it is set to 'No Access' or 'System Email' only. The Email Logs can provide information on whether the email was sent or an error was encountered in the delivery.

Email invalidation can also prevent production users from receiving messages generated from the sandbox. When a sandbox is created or refreshed, the email address name@email.com becomes name@email.com.invalid. The administrator should check and make sure that the target users have the correct email address.

There are no specific logs named 'System Log' and 'Workflow Log'.

Objective: Testing, Debugging, and Deployment
Detailed Objective: Describe the environments, requirements, and process for deploying code and associated configurations.

Question 9 Answer:
C. Outbound Message

Outbound messaging uses the notifications() call to send SOAP messages over HTTP(S) to a designated endpoint when triggered by a workflow rule or record-triggered flow. After setting up outbound messaging, when a triggering event occurs, a message is sent to the specified endpoint URL. The message contains the fields specified when the outbound message was created. Once the endpoint URL receives the message, it can take the information from the message and process it.

If a pure declarative solution is required for outbound messaging, a flow or workflow rule can be used since other tools like Process Builder need to invoke Apex code to do the same.

Objective: Process Automation and Logic
Detailed Objective: Describe the capabilities of the declarative process automation features.

Question 10 Answer:
A. Code is developed locally and Apex tests can be initialized from Visual Studio Code
B. Each developer can define their own set of metadata files to include in a local project

Each developer can define their own set of metadata components to include in a local project by configuring the manifest file (package.xml). Changes made to metadata files are performed locally (regardless of the org edition) through the code editor and are deployed to an authorized org using Salesforce CLI commands either directly or indirectly. Apex tests in an org can also be run from Visual Studio Code using Salesforce CLI.

Question 11 Answer:
C. Staging

The staging environment is the last environment in the development lifecycle before production. The staging sandbox is a Full sandbox that contains all data and metadata that's in production. It's a full replica of production that enables users to perform real-world testing and catch any data-dependent issues that affect the behavior of the app. The staging environment can be used to perform a test deployment and final regression, test run all tests, and make sure that the deployment is successful.

Question 12 Answer:
B. Configure the record-triggered flow to access and compare the old and new values of the field and conditionally invoke methods.
A record-triggered flow that is configured to run when a record is created/updated, or updated only, is capable of accessing the previous values of the record that triggered the flow using the $Record__Prior global variable. By comparing the old and new values of the record using the $Record__Prior and $Record global variables, logic can be implemented to execute invocable methods accordingly using a Decision element.

Although Apex trigger or Process Builder can also be used to meet the goal, they are not necessary since the existing flow is capable of meeting the requirement. An Assignment element is not required in order to access old and new values of the record. In this scenario, Formula resources can be created and used in a Decision element to branch out to the different actions accordingly.

Question 13 Answer:
A. Committing changes to a Salesforce org
D. Accessing code coverage test results for an Apex class
E. Using ApexLog to access a debug log

Tooling API can be used for fine-grained access to an org's metadata. Its main use cases include source control integration, continuous integration, and deployment of Apex classes and triggers. Some specific tasks that can be accomplished using Tooling API are accessing a debug log, accessing code coverage results for an Apex class, and committing changes to a Salesforce org.

For simple migrations using an XML file, or retrieving, deploying, creating, updating, or deleting metadata such as the definition of a custom object, Metadata API is typically used.

Question 14 Answer:
A. Data import
B. Bulk Force.com API calls
D. Mass actions

Bulk triggers can handle both single record updates and bulk operations like: Data import, Force.com Bulk API calls & Mass actions. Lightning events and Visualforce actions both depend on a controller that should still utilize the use of Apex DML statements.

Question 15 Answer:
C. Lookup

A lookup relationship allows objects to be loosely related and allows independent record ownership.

Objective: Data Modeling and Management
Detailed Objective: Given a set of requirements, determine, create, and access the appropriate data model including objects, fields, and relationships.

Question 16 Answer:
A. "New Document" will be printed in the log.

'New Document' will be printed in the log but not 'No Title' since the value of the 'title' variable is already defined through the property definition.

The implementing class can also define other methods in addition to the implemented methods required by the interface. If the method signature has an argument, the implementing method must also have the same argument and data type. However, the argument name can differ since it is only a variable name.

Question 17 Answer:
D. Value of gradeEqual = D

Since there is no ELSE statement in the code, the IF statements will continue to be evaluated, even if one of the conditions is met. Since the value of testRawScore (75) is greater than 70, the code within the third IF statement assigns the value 'C' to the 'gradeEqual' variable. But since 75 is also greater than 60, the last IF statement assigns the value 'D' to the 'gradeEqual' variable, replacing the prior value. As a result, the final value of the variable is 'D'.

Question 18 Answer:
A. It has an event-driven architecture
B. It is device-aware and supports cross-browser compatibility

Lightning Component uses an event-driven architecture for better decoupling between components. Any component can subscribe to an application event, or to a component event they can see. The Lightning Component framework supports the latest in browser technology such as HTML5, CSS3, and touch events and includes responsive components.

Converting Visualforce pages and components to Lightning components requires manual work. Aside from the Aura Components model, the Lightning Web Component model can also be used to build Lightning components.

Question 19 Answer:
B. Results were evenly distributed among the objects returned.

If a limit is set on the entire query, results are evenly distributed among the objects returned. Limits can also be set per individual object.

Question 20 Answer:
C. SELECT LeadSource, COUNT(Name) FROM Lead GROUP BY LeadSource

A GROUP BY clause can be used with COUNT(fieldName) to allow analyzing records and returning summary reporting information.

Question 21 Answer:
A. Accounts using the values of related opportunities
B. Opportunities using the values of opportunity products related to the opportunity
D. Campaigns using the values of campaign member custom fields

Roll-up summary fields are used to display a calculated value of related records. The roll-up summary field can be created on any object on the Master side of a Master-Detail relationship. Since Case records are related to Accounts and Contacts via lookup relationships, they cannot be used in roll-up summary fields on those two objects.

There are some special scenarios where roll-up summary fields can be used in a lookup relationship, namely Opportunity-Opportunity Product, Account-Opportunity, and Campaign-Campaign Member.

Question 22 Answer:
C. Change its own field values using trigger.new.
D. Create a validation before accepting own field changes.

Changing own field values can be done on trigger.new before the DML operation is committed. Before Update triggers can also be used to validate own field values before accepting change by evaluating the field and then throw an error if necessary using the addError() method.

Trigger.old is always read-only and Trigger.new cannot be deleted.

Question 23 Answer:
B. SELECT Name, (SELECT Tracking_Number__c FROM Shipments__r) FROM Sales_Order__c

Parent-child relationships can be traversed in the SELECT clause of a SOQL query by using a nested query. In this case, Shipments__r is the name of the relationship that the parent object named \'Sales_Order__c\' has with the child object named \'Shipment__c\'.

Question 24 Answer:
A. Use a switch block with multiple values

The "switch" control flow statement is capable of handling multiple values in its "when" block as well as ENUM values. By converting the if-else statement into this structure, code becomes easier to read. Also, in the "switch" control flow statement, the variable name doesn\'t need to be repeated which helps reduce code size relatively.

Using nested "if-else" statements nor splitting the code block into separate "if" statements only breaks the necessary logic in this scenario and does not help meet the requirement. Using a switch with single values may make it readable, but it does not help reduce code size.

Question 25 Answer:
A. The 'with sharing' keywords
D. The 'inherited sharing' keywords

Either 'with sharing' or 'inherited sharing' can be used in the definition of the custom controller class to ensure that it respects the running user's organization-wide defaults, role hierarchy, and sharing rules when displaying a Visualforce page. Using an explicit sharing declaration ensures that only records that the running user has sharing access to are displayed.

Access modifiers are used to define the scope of the methods and variables that are created within an Apex class. They are not used to define sharing settings. Also, a 'sharing' or 'protected' access modifier does not exist.

Question 26 Answer:
C. While creating a sandbox, an option to use an existing sandbox can be selected.
D. A sandbox can be cloned to ensure that the same metadata components are available for other developers.

It is possible to clone a sandbox by clicking 'Clone' next to the name of a completed sandbox. An existing sandbox can also be cloned by selecting it from the 'Create From' drop-down menu. Instead of downloading and installing an AppExchange solution for this use case, it is better to use native functionality. Also, a change set is used to migrate metadata components from one related environment to another, but this use case requires reducing the amount of time spent by developers on migrating metadata components, for which cloning is an appropriate solution.

Question 27 Answer:
A. {! account.contacts }

When using a Standard Account Controller, the current record is accessed as {! account }. One parent-to-child relationship level can be traversed by using the child relationship name, in this case {! account.contacts }. This markup accesses the list of child contacts, which can be iterated upon.

<apex:repeat> is the markup used to iterate over a list, not to access a list of child records.
The markup {! contacts } would only be valid if there were contact variables in a controller extension associated with the page (or in a Custom Controller if the Standard Controller were not being used). A for loop is used in Apex, and is not Visualforce markup. Also, this.contacts would not automatically exist; it would have to be queried.

Question 28 Answer:
A. Anonymous blocks can include user-defined methods
B. If the APEX code completes successfully, data changes are automatically committed

Anonymous blocks always run as the current user. Anonymous blocks can be compiled and executed using the Developer Console, Visual Studio Code, or via a SOAP API call. The Tooling API can also be used to execute anonymous blocks via REST calls.

Question 29 Answer:
C. Each outcome in the element should be configured to execute 'only if the record that triggered the flow to run is updated to meet the condition requirements'.

When configuring an outcome in the 'Decision' element of a flow, the following two options are available for executing the outcome:

1) If the condition requirements are met
2) Only if the record that triggered the flow to run is updated to meet the condition requirements

The first option executes the outcome if the condition requirements are met regardless of the previous and new field values, except when the 'Is Changed' operator is used. The second option allows executing the outcome only if the record changes from not meeting the condition requirements to meeting them. This option, which is similar to the 'Is Changed' operator, can be used to execute an outcome only if the value of a field changes. It can be used for this requirement to execute two different outcomes based on whether the value of the 'Rating' field changes to 'Hot' or 'Cold'. Note that when the 'Is Changed' operator is selected, the 'When to Execute Outcome' setting will be automatically set and fixed to 'If the condition requirements are met'.

A $CHANGED global variable in Flow Builder does not exist. It is not necessary to create a custom field since the $Record__Prior global variable in Flow Builder can be used to access previous field values of the updated record.

Question 30 Answer:
B. An access modifier is required in the declaration of a top-level class
C. A developer may add optional extensions and/or implementations.
E. The keyword [class] followed by the name of the class is necessary

To define a class, an access modifier (such as public or global) must be used in the declaration of a top-level class. An access modifier is not required in the declaration of an inner class. Definition modifiers (such as virtual, abstract) are optional. Whether an access modifier has been specified or not, the keyword [class] is always mandatory.

Question 31 Answer:
B. getProductList

A Visualforce controller class provides developers a way of displaying data and other computed values in the page markup. These methods are called getter methods, which use the case-insensitive naming convention 'getIdentifier', where 'get' is a name prefix and 'Identifier' is the name of the variable that will be specified in the Visualforce page markup. Therefore, if 'productList' is the variable name in the page markup such as in the above scenario, then its corresponding getter method should be defined as 'getProductList'.

Question 32 Answer:
A. Edit
D. View

Visualforce overrides are supported for new, edit, view, tab, list, and clone actions in Lightning console apps. They are not currently supported for delete and custom actions.

Question 33 Answer:
A. Formula Field

Formula fields allow inserting references to fields of a parent object. For example, Account.Stock_Symbol__c

Roll-Up Summary fields aggregates value from children records to the parent record. Lookup fields are used in establishing a lookup relationship between two objects. This scenario does not require Apex code since a formula field is sufficient.

Question 34 Answer:
C. Return type

The data type of the value returned by an Apex method is required; the void return type can be used if the method does not return a value.

Access modifiers such as 'public' or 'protected' are optional. Definition modifiers such as 'virtual' and 'abstract' are optional for defining an Apex class or method. A list of input parameters can be specified for a method. The parameters should be enclosed in parentheses and separated by commas, each preceded by its data type. If there are no parameters, an empty set of parentheses can be used.

Question 35 Answer:
B. public static Boolean method(String param) { ... }

The proper syntax of declaring a method in Apex is:

[public | private | protected | global] [override] [static] return_data_type method_name(param_data_type1 param_name1, ...)

An access modifier such as public, or private, is used but optional depending on the requirement. The override keyword can be added to the declaration to override methods in a class that has been defined as virtual or abstract. The static keyword can be used to enable the method to be called without instantiating the class. If the method returns a value, the data type of the returned value must be specified before the method name. Otherwise, the void keyword is used. Enclosed in parentheses, input parameters are separated by commas where each is preceded by its data type. If a method does not have parameters, an empty set of parentheses is used.

Question 36 Answer:
D. The String will be passed by value and the List will be passed by reference.

When working with Visualforce, or Apex methods, in particular, primitive types such as Strings are passed by value to a controller, while non-primitive types such as Lists are passed by reference. This allows the controller to act directly on non-primitive types and change the underlying data.

Question 37 Answer:
B. A Visualforce page's functionality needs to run in system mode.
C. The functionality of the standard controller of the Visualforce page needs to be replaced.

A custom controller is an Apex class that implements all of the logic for a page without leveraging a standard controller. Custom controllers run entirely in system mode, which does not enforce the permissions and field-level security of the current user.

A custom controller is not required to override the save action, a controller extension can be used to override one or more actions such as edit, view, save, or delete, and add new actions beyond a standard controller.

SALESFORCE CERTIFIED PLATFORM DEVELOPER I - RAPID CERTIFICATION EXAM PREP GUIDE

Question 38 Answer:
B. Every DML statement executed in any of the 3 triggers will count toward the overall limit within a single transaction
D. Calls to Approval.process() will count toward the DML limit

DML Limits apply across the full span of a transaction, so all 3 triggers will share the pool of available limits. DML statements should never be put inside loops because they will execute once for each loop iteration. Instead, processing loops should build up a list of records which would then be updated outside of the loop.

In addition to traditional DML statements such as insert, update, upsert, delete, undelete, and merge, certain method calls such as Approval.process(), Database.convertLead(), Database.emptyRecycleBin(), Database.rollback(), Database.setSavePoint(), EventBus.publish(), and System.runAs() also count toward the DML transaction limit.

Question 39 Answer:
A. CSS files
B. images
C. JavaScript files

The $ContentAsset global value provider is used for referencing images, stylesheets, and JavaScript files in a Lightning component. It allows the developer to load an asset by name instead of using file paths or URLs. It is not used for loading HTML files or referencing font files.

Question 40 Answer:
D. Model View Controller

Visualforce uses the traditional model-view-controller (MVC) paradigm, with the option to use auto-generated controllers for database objects, providing simple and tight integration with the database.

Question 41 Answer:
B. getLabel()

The getLabel() method of the DescribeSObjectResult class returns the object's label, which may or may not match the object name.

Question 42 Answer:
A. Map<ID, String> sampleMap;
B. Boolean y;
D. String a,b,c;

Currency is not a valid Apex data type. Instead, the Decimal type is used. Also, Number is not a valid data type. Integer, Long, Decimal and Double are primitive data types available to use when working with numbers or numeric values.

Question 43 Answer:
B. Create a User trace flag.

A User trace flag should be created to activate a debug log for the user's session. Once created, events that will be generated by the user based on the Debug Log Level assigned to the user trace flag will be stored in a debug log. The debug log can then be used for identifying and troubleshooting the issue.

Apex class and trigger trace flags do not cause debug logs to be created. They are only created to override existing logging levels. A Debug Session trace flag does not exist.

Question 44 Answer:
B. When a many-to-many relationship is defined between objects A and B using a junction object, data from the junction object can appear in a related list on the page layouts of objects A and B
D. When a lookup relationship to (parent) object B is defined on (child) object A, data from object A can appear as a related list on page layouts of object B

When a lookup relationship is defined, data from the lookup object can be displayed in a custom related list on the other object. For example, if a custom object named Schedule is related to a custom object called Training Course, a list of related Schedule records can be displayed on the Training Course record page.

When a many-to-many relationship is defined, data from a junction object can be displayed on page layouts for either object.

Question 45 Answer:
A. View information about all the completed Apex jobs by navigating to 'Apex Jobs' in Setup.
C. View information about all the future jobs that are scheduled to run by navigating to 'Scheduled Jobs' in Setup.

All completed Apex jobs, irrespective of the nature of the job, can be viewed by navigating to 'Apex Jobs' in Setup. This page can be accessed to view any information about Apex jobs. Since the job is scheduled to run at a particular time, the status of the scheduled job already run, and information about jobs waiting to run next can be viewed by navigating to 'Scheduled Jobs' in Setup. Checking this information can help determine if the scheduled batch classes are recurring properly, and should be part of the diagnosis.

There is no 'Jobs' page in Setup. Information about a scheduled batch class with future method cannot appear on the 'Apex Flex Queue' page since future jobs are currently not supported by Apex Flex Queue.

Question 46 Answer:
D. The flow should use a record variable named 'recordId' that is available for input.

To meet this requirement, a record variable named 'recordId' should be created in the flow. This variable should be available for input. The quick action on the Lightning page would automatically pass the record into this record variable. The flow can access the variable to get the required information for sending an email. It is not necessary to add the 'Get Records' element to the flow to get the warehouse record. An Apex action is also unnecessary to meet the requirement. The Lightning page does not need to be edited to enable passing the record. That would only be required if the flow was embedded on the Lightning page using Lightning App Builder.

Question 47 Answer:
A. It can be used to allow 'list controllers' similar to pre-built Visualforce list controllers to be created.
C. It can be used to allow 'pre-built list controllers' to be extended
E. It can be used for mass updates.

StandardSetController objects can allow the creation of list controllers similar to, or as extensions of, the pre-built Visualforce list controllers provided by Salesforce. StandardSetController is useful for writing pages that will perform mass updates.

The maximum record limit for StandardSetController is 10,000 records. If a query locator is used for instantiating the StandardSetController to return more than 10,000 records, then a LimitException will be thrown. However, instantiating StandardSetController with a list of more than 10,000 records will not throw an exception, and instead trims the records down to the limit.

Question 48 Answer:
B. Create a flow with Flow Builder

A flow can be used to create a wizard-like interface where details can be entered on one screen and a calculation displayed on the next screen. Visualforce is not necessary as the requirement can be met by a declarative solution. Neither approval workflows nor Process Builder can be used for building interfaces.

Question 49 Answer:
C. Suspend the subscription of the Apex trigger to the platform event.

The Apex trigger needs to stop executing to prevent further issues in the org without losing any published event messages. To achieve this, the subscription of the trigger to the platform event can be suspended, which in this state, does not invoke the trigger to process any published event messages. The subscription can be resumed to either start with the earliest unprocessed event message when the subscription was suspended or process new event messages only.

Deactivating the Apex trigger or storing published event messages in a custom object is not required. Pausing the publishing of event messages is also not required and may not be feasible. Scheduling the receipt of platform event messages is not possible.

Question 50 Answer:
C. SVG File

The SVG file contains custom icon resource for components used in the Lightning App Builder or Experience Builder. SVG stands for Scalable Vector Graphics. A developer may also utilize more of SVG usage by using the Salesforce Lightning Design System.

Question 51 Answer:
A. Creating a custom object
B. Deleting a custom object
C. Creating lookup and master-detail relationships

Using schema builder, objects and relationships can be defined. Custom objects can be created and deleted. It cannot be used to export or import schema definition.

Question 52 Answer:
B. The CSS file is used to style the component and match the company's branding guidelines
C. The JavaScript file defines how the component UI reacts to client events
D. The HTML file defines the UI structure of the component

The HTML file is the basis for the UI of the component. Hence, it contains the UI structure. The JavaScript file defines the HTML element provided in the HTML file including event handling and the core logic. The CSS file is used to style the component using standard CSS.

The configuration file is used to define metadata values of the component. It is not used for fetching data. Retrieving data will require server-side controllers to perform such a task. Also, the test files contained in a Lightning web component directory are run using Jest, which is a third-party testing framework used for testing JavaScript code. These test files are not uploaded to the Salesforce org and are only run locally.

Question 53 Answer:
A. Class-based
D. Trigger-based
E. User-based

Debug logs can be set up for specific users, Apex classes, and Apex triggers. In addition, Automated Process and Platform Integration are also available entity types.

Neither Query-based nor JavaScript-based trace flags exist.

Question 54 Answer:
   A. Map<Id,Schema.RecordTypeInfo> mapRecTypes = result.getRecordTypeInfosById();

To return a map of the record Ids and details of their associated record types, the getRecordTypeInfosById() method of the Schema.DescribeSObjectResult class can be used. The data type used to store the results of this method is a map collection in which the key is an Id and the value is the Schema.RecordTypeInfo class.

The 'getRecordTypeInfos' method returns a list of the record types, but since line 6 contains code that uses the get() method, a method that returns a map should be used. There are no methods called 'getRecordTypes' and 'getRecordTypeIds'.

Question 55 Answer:
A. For(Type variable: listOrSet) loop

While-Do is an invalid loop. Although a While, Do-While or For (initialize; condition; increment) loop can be used to traverse through a list or set, the size of the collection will need to be explicitly determined by calling the size() method, which does not conform to the context of the question where the size of the collection is supposedly unknown.

A For (Type variable: listOrSet) loop will naturally traverse through the collection without having to take note of its size. The Type of the variable in the variable definition should be the same as the Type of the member in the list or set.

Question 56 Answer:
A. The helper file

The helper file is the most appropriate place to put functions that can be called by any JavaScript code in a component bundle. The component file contains the markup for the component, while the controller file contains functions that are typically called as a result of a browser or platform event. The design file exposes attributes of the component that can be modified from an interface such as Lightning App Builder.

Question 57 Answer:
B. Standard Page Layout
C. Navigation Bar
D. Custom App

A developer can display a Visualforce Page from the App Launcher, add a Visualforce Page to the Navigation Bar, display a Visualforce Page within a Standard Page Layout, and launch a Visualforce Page as a Quick Action by overriding Buttons or Links.

Question 58 Answer:
C. <apex:dataTable>
D. <apex:pageBlockTable>

Iteration components work on a collection of items instead of a single value. <apex:pageBlockTable> is a type of iteration component that can be used to generate a table of data, complete with platform styling. The <apex:dataTable> component can be used if custom styling is required.

<apex:table> and <apex:outputTable> are not valid components.

Question 59 Answer:
A. Validation Rule

A validation rule can be used to ensure that the code entered is valid. In this particular scenario, the validation rule's formula field can contain a list of ISO codes with which to verify the country code.

There is no need for programmatic customization in this case as a declarative tool can meet the requirement. Workflow rules cannot be used to perform data validation.

Question 60 Answer:
A. No parent or child cases will be created.
D. The trigger will be recursively called and result in an infinite loop.

The code consists of an 'after insert' trigger which contains a DML statement that inserts records of the same object. The DML statement will recursively invoke the trigger, resulting in an infinite loop, and eventually throw an exception. As a result, no parent or child cases will be created. To prevent trigger recursion, a static boolean variable can be used in the trigger helper class to make the trigger only run once per transaction.

SAMPLE EXAM II (60 questions, 105 minutes)

Question 1:
Which of the following provides a dynamic environment for viewing and modifying objects and relationships?
Choose 1 answer.

A. Schema Builder
B. Flows
C. Process Builder
D. Process Visualizer
E. Approval Visualizer

Question 2:
Given the following Visualforce page snippet, which of the following statements are true?
Choose 3 answers.

```
<apex:page standardController="Lead" extensions="LeadExtA, LeadExtB, LeadExtC">
   <apex:outputText value="{!display}" />
</apex:page>
```

A. It is possible to have multiple extensions on a single Visualforce page, and extensions can be reused on different pages.
B. LeadExtA, LeadExtB, or LeadExtC cannot be used without the 'Lead' standard controller.
C. If a method is declared across all extensions, LeadExtC will override all methods.
D. The <apex:outputText> component will not render any value since {$ } notation is not used.
E. LeadExtA, LeadExtB, and LeadExtC are controller extensions used by the Visualforce page.

Question 3:
Unit tests for Apex classes are used not just to be able to deploy to production but also to provide confirmation that an Apex class is working as expected. What is the proper method to properly create an Apex Unit Test?
Choose 1 answer.

A. Annotate @SeeAllData=true on the test class. Execute the methods to be tested and verify the results using System.debug();
B. Query test data on the organization. Execute the methods to be tested and verify the expected results using assertions.
C. Annotate @SeeAllData=true on the test class. Execute the methods to be tested and verify the results using assertions.
D. Create valid test data for testing. Execute the methods to be tested and verify the expected results using assertions.

Question 4:
A developer at Cosmic Solutions is creating a Visualforce page to render a table of cases. He is considering the use of a Standard List Controller to avoid unnecessarily building a custom controller. Which of the following are benefits of Standard List Controllers?
Choose 3 answers.

A. Records can be dynamically sorted by rendered fields
B. A dynamic number of records can be rendered on the page
C. Pagination of records
D. Simple calculations can be applied before saving
E. Existing List View filters can be applied

Question 5:
As a customer developing a new force.com application that will include Apex code, what considerations are valid?
Choose 2 answers.

A. It is a best practice to have separate development and testing environments
B. It is required that development, testing, and production are in separate environments
C. At least 2 environments are required
D. Development and testing can be performed directly in the production environment

Question 6:

A developer has created the following 'before update' trigger on the Opportunity object to update the value of a field on any newly updated opportunities automatically:

What will be the value of the Status__c field if a sales representative wins a sales deal and closes the corresponding opportunity record in Salesforce?

Choose 1 answer.

```
trigger OpportunityTrigger on Opportunity (before update) {

    for (Opportunity opp : Trigger.new) {

        switch on opp.StageName {
            when 'New' {
                opp.Status__c = 'New';
            }
            when 'Closed Won' {
                opp.Status__c = 'Order Required';
            }
            when 'Closed Lost' {
                opp.Status__c = 'Cancelled';
            }
            when else {
                opp.Status__c = 'Awaiting Closure';
            }
        }

    }

}
```

A. Closed Won
B. Awaiting Closure
C. Closed
D. Order Required

Question 7:
A developer working for Cosmic Solutions would like to propagate the deletion of a custom object from a developer sandbox to the production org used by the company. Which Salesforce feature or tool can be used for this requirement?
Choose 1 answer.

A. Data Loader
B. Ant Migration Tool
C. Change Set
D. Unmanaged Package

Question 8:
Cosmic Solutions developers each work in their own developer sandbox to deploy user stories. When their stories are ready to test, they check in all metadata necessary to deploy the change as a functional unit into a source control provider. The source control server has a monitor that checks for changes and automatically moves them to an integration sandbox. If conflicts between 2 files are detected, a message is sent to the owners of the files so the merge conflict can be resolved. As each self-contained unit of functionality passes internal testing, it is promoted into a sandbox for client testing. What development model is this an example of?
Choose 1 answer.

A. Salesforce CLI
B. Package Development
C. Change Set Development
D. Org Development

Question 9:
A developer is creating a simple calculator using a Visualforce page that will have 2 numerical input fields and perform an arithmetic operation based on the user input. What method should the developer use in order to process and calculate the input of the user in the controller?
Choose 1 answer.

A. Process Method
B. Input Method
C. Setter Method
D. Pass Method

Question 10:
What attribute should the developer use to render a Visualforce page as a PDF file?
Choose 1 answer.

A. docType='pdf-1.0-strict'
B. contentType='application/vnd.pdf'
C. docType='pdf-5.0'
D. renderAs='pdf'

Question 11:
What trigger context variable returns true if the current context for the Apex code is a trigger, and not a Visualforce page, a Web service, or an executeanonymous() API call?
Choose 1 answer.

A. isUpdate
B. isUndelete
C. isExecuting
D. oldMap

Question 12:
A developer would like to use the following SOSL query in an Apex class to search for a keyword. Which data type should be used to store the result returned by the query?
Choose 1 answer.

FIND 'New York' IN ALL FIELDS RETURNING Account, Contact
A. Map<Account, Contact>
B. Map<Id, Contact>
C. List<sObject>
D. List<List<sObject>>

Question 13:
Which of the following are valid assignment statements?
Choose 2 answers.

A. Long num = 1.2345;
B. Double num = 1234.5;
C. Decimal num = 12345;
D. Integer num = 123.45;

Question 14:
A Salesforce developer noticed that an Apex method used in their custom Contact management application has been throwing null pointer exceptions on certain occasions. Upon investigating, it was identified that the error was due to code that accesses the Account field of a Contact record, which is not associated with an account, and executes the 'isSet' method on the Account sObject. Given a snippet of the code below, which of the following options can be used to avoid the exception?
Choose 1 answer.

public static void assignPrimaryContact() {

   Contact con = getContact();
   Boolean hasAssigned = con.Account.isSet('Has_Primary_Contact__c ');
   // ...
}

   A. Boolean hasAssigned = getContact().Account:Account.Has_Primary_Contact__c?null;
   B. Boolean hasAssigned = getContact().Account.?isSet('Has_Primary_Contact__c ');
   C. Boolean hasAssigned = getContact().Account?Account.Has_Primary_Contact__c:null;
   D. Boolean hasAssigned = getContact().Account?.isSet('Has_Primary_Contact__c ');

Question 15:
A PageReference is a reference to an instantiation of a page. Which of the following are valid means of referencing or instantiating a PageReference?
Choose 2 answers.

A. PageReference.page('URL');
B. ApexPages.Page().existingPageName;
C. Page.existingPageName;
D. PageReference pageRef = new PageReference('URL');

Question 16:
Which of the following are part of the control layer in the MVC model?
Choose 2 answers.

A. Apex custom controllers
B. Visualforce Controllers
C. List Views
D. Apps

Question 17:
A developer would like to insert hundreds of contacts that have been obtained from an external system. These contact records should be related to specific account records in Salesforce which also exist in the external system. However, since the external system does not contain information about record identifiers associated with account records in Salesforce, the .csv file that contains the contact records does not contain parent account IDs. What should the developer do to ensure that the contact records are related to their parent account records after the import process?
Choose 2 answers.

A. Develop a custom integration in the external system that obtains account record IDs from Salesforce regularly.
B. Define a Unique External ID field on the Account object and populate it with unique record identifiers from the external system.
C. Add unique record identifiers from the account records in the external system to the .csv file and use it to insert the new records.
D. Create an Apex trigger that automatically relates inserted contact records to account records in Salesforce.

Question 18:
Which of the following are valid considerations that a new developer should be aware of when developing in a multi-tenant environment?
Choose 2 answers.

A. Many customers share the same instance, so queries need to ensure the correct organization id is referenced to return the correct organizational data
B. The number of API calls allowed is unlimited
C. Governor limits ensure that the amount of CPU time is monitored and limited per customer over a defined time period to ensure that performance in one org is not impacted by another
D. Restrictions are enforced on code that can be deployed into a production environment

Question 19:
Which of the following can be uploaded as a static resource and can be referenced in a Visualforce page using a global variable?
Choose 3 answers.

A. Archive
B. Apex Class
C. Style Sheet
D. JavaScript File
E. Apex Trigger

Question 20:
A developer is required to embed a website into a Visualforce page. What Visualforce component can the developer use?
Choose 1 answer.

A. <apex:include>
B. <apex:iframe>
C. <apex:getsite>

Question 21:
Given the sample log excerpt below, which line(s) correspond to an execution unit of a debug log?
20:43:45.1 (1707921) | EXECUTION_STARTED
20:43:45.1 (1714356) | CODE_UNIT_STARTED | [EXTERNAL] | 01pO0000000Hury | LeadBLTest.setUpTestData
20:43:51.574 (7549778580) | CODE_UNIT_FINISHED | LeadBLTest.setUpTestData
20:43:51.574 (7550987692) | EXECUTION_FINISHED
Choose 1 answer.

A. 1st & 2nd
B. 1st, 2nd, 3rd, & 4th
C. 4th only
D. 2nd only

Question 22:
Which of the following types of methods in a custom controller support the use of DML statements such as insert and update?
Choose 2 answers.

A. Constructors
B. Static methods
C. Getter methods
D. Setter methods

Question 23:
A developer is going through the Visualforce pages created in his company's org to identify and fix any potential vulnerabilities. One of the pages uses a static HTML file that has been downloaded from a third-party source. If 'resource_name' refers to the name that was specified when the file was uploaded as a static resource, which of the following should the developer use to reference the file on a separate domain and improve security?
Choose 1 answer.

A. $Resource.<resource_name>
B. $IFrameResource.<resource_name>
C. $IFrame.<resource_name>
D. $Library.<resource_name>

Question 24:
Which of the following statements about running Apex test classes in the Developer Console are true?
Choose 3 answers.

A. The [New Suite] option is used to create multiple test classes at the same time.
B. The [Suite Manager] option is used to abort the test selected in the Tests tab.
C. The [Rerun Failed Tests] option reruns only the failed tests from the test run that are highlighted in the Tests tab.
D. If the test run includes more than one test class, the Developer Console always runs tests asynchronously in the background.
E. An Overall Code Coverage pane is available that displays the percentage of code coverage for each class in org.

Question 25:
Kate, the Director of Operations at Cosmic Solutions, is concerned that critical cases are not being handled properly. She wants to be notified whenever Customer Support management approves a Case to be flagged 'Critical', so that she can monitor its progress. A Salesforce Administrator has been asked to use In-App Notifications to alert Kate about these cases. Which of the following automation features could be used to send Kate Custom Notifications?
Choose 2 answers.

A. Approval Process
B. Flow
C. Workflow Rule
D. Process Builder

Question 26:
A delivery company uses Salesforce REST API to publish platform event messages for providing its B2B clients with real-time information on the status of their deliveries. Cosmic Furniture uses Salesforce to manage its business operations and has hired the services of the delivery company. It would like to automatically update related sales records when the delivery company publishes a platform event message. Which of the following should be done to meet the requirement?
Choose 2 answers.

A. Use CometD to subscribe to the platform event published by the delivery company.
B. Create an Apex trigger to subscribe to the platform event and update records.
C. Create a platform event-triggered flow and specify the platform event.
D. Use the $Record global variable to access field values in the event message.

Question 27:
Which of the following is the correct syntax for a try-catch-finally block?
Choose 1 answer.

A. try { *code here* } catch (Exception e) { *code here* } finally { *code here* }
B. catch (Exception e) { *code here* } try { *code here* } finally { *code here* }
C. finally { *code here* } catch { *code here* } try { *code here* }
D. try { *code here* } finally { *code here* } catch (Exception e) { *code here* }

Question 28:
Because Apex runs in a multitenant environment, the Apex runtime engine enforces limits to ensure that Apex code or processes don't monopolize shared resources. What are valid examples of these limits?
Choose 3 answers.

A. Total number of records retrieved by SOQL queries
B. CPU time per transaction
C. Time executing a SOQL query
D. Maximum number of records that can be stored
E. Maximum execution time for a DML operation

Question 29:
What will happen if a governor limit is hit from an Apex class that was called from an Apex controller class of a Visualforce page?
Choose 2 answers.

A. It will rollback all changes made up to the error.
B. It will save all changes made from the Apex class.
C. It will save all changes made from the Apex controller class.
D. An exception will be thrown.

Question 30:
What is true regarding a future method?
Choose 2 answers.

A. Methods that are annotated with @future identify methods that are executed asynchronously.
B. Methods that are annotated with @future identify methods that are executed synchronously.
C. A method annotated with @future can call another method that also has the @future annotation.
D. Methods annotated with @future can only return a void type.

Question 31:
The Salesforce Administrator at Cosmic Mobile has configured the Next Best Action component to display recommendations to its customer service representatives (CSRs) regarding phone plans. When a CSR accepts a recommendation for a customer who wants to upgrade to a certain plan, a flow is launched to process the upgrade. If the offer is rejected, the flow needs to perform a different action. How can a Salesforce Administrator meet this requirement?
Choose 2 answers.

A. Create a flow to run when a recommendation is accepted and another one for when it is rejected
B. Select the flows to invoke in the recommendation settings for acceptance and rejection accordingly
C. Enable 'Launch Flow on Rejection' for the Next Best Action component in Lightning App Builder
D. Build a single flow to perform an action that is used when a recommendation is accepted or rejected

Question 32:
A Salesforce Administrator is considering whether to use a lookup or master-detail relationship. Which of the following are capabilities of a lookup relationship but not a master-detail relationship?
Choose 2 answers.

A. The related record can have a different owner than the parent record.
B. The lookup field does not need to be a required field on the page layout.
C. Roll-up summary fields can be added to the parent master object.
D. When a parent record is deleted, the child record is always deleted.

Question 33:
A developer is unable to delete a custom field as it is referenced somewhere in Salesforce. Which of the following might contain the conflicting reference?
Choose 3 answers.

A. Formula field
B. Workflow Field Update
C. Dynamic SOQL
D. Apex Class
E. Email Template

Question 34:
Cosmic Lights uses the standard Contact object to store information about people associated with B2B companies who purchase the products manufactured by the company. A custom object is used to store information about sales orders. When a person associated with a company purchases a product, a custom field on that person's contact record is updated by a salesperson manually. When this field is updated, a Salesforce survey should be sent to the person to gather certain information, such as the reason behind the purchase and how their previous purchases influenced the recent purchase decision. What solution should be recommended to meet this requirement?
Choose 1 answer.

A. Create a process using Process Builder that executes an action type called 'Send Survey Invitation' when the value of the custom field changes.
B. Create an outbound message that is sent to a third-party survey application when the value of the custom field changes.
C. Create an Apex trigger that sends a survey invitation to the contact when the value of the custom field changes.
D. Create a flow that sends a survey invitation to the contact automatically when the value of the custom field changes.

Question 35:
A developer from Cosmic Solutions needs to retrieve subquery results from a SOQL query if the result is not empty. Which lines in the given options can be used to replace the comments in the code snippet to accomplish the task?
Choose 2 answers.

```
public class QueryHelper {
   public static List<Opportunity> getOpps(String industry) {
      List<Account> accts = [SELECT Id, (SELECT Id, Name FROM Opportunities) FROM Account WHERE Industry =: industry];
      List<Opportunity> opps = new List<Opportunity>();
      for (Account a : accts) {
         if (/* Check if the subquery result is not empty */) {
            /* Retrieve the subquery result and add to the opportunity list opps */
         }
      }
      return opps;
   }
}
```

A. !a.Opportunities.isEmpty()
B. a.Opportunity.isNotEmpty()
C. opps.add(a.Opportunity);
D. opps.addAll(a.Opportunities);

Question 36:
An assignment statement is any statement that places a value into a variable. Which one of the following expressions is a valid Apex assignment statement?
Choose 1 answer.

A. Account acc = new Account();
B. Map<Id, Account> = [SELECT Id, Name FROM Account];
C. List<Contact> conList = new [SELECT Id FROM Contact];
D. String a = new String('sampleString');

Question 37:
Which of the following queries show valid syntax for querying data from related standard objects?
Choose 2 answers.

A. SELECT Id, (SELECT Name, BillingState FROM Account WHERE Account.BillingState=\'Arizona\') FROM Contact LIMIT 50
B. SELECT Name, Contact.LastName, Contact.FirstName FROM Account WHERE BillingState=\'Arizona\' LIMIT 50
C. SELECT Name, (SELECT LastName, FirstName FROM Contact) FROM Account WHERE BillingState=\'Arizona\' LIMIT 50
D. SELECT Account.Name, Account.BillingState FROM Contact WHERE Account.BillingState=\'Arizona\' LIMIT 50
E. SELECT Name, (SELECT LastName, FirstName FROM Contacts) FROM Account WHERE BillingState=\'Arizona\' LIMIT 50

Question 38:
A developer has written a code block that does not include the with/without sharing keyword. Which of the following will use the sharing settings, field permissions, and Organization-Wide Defaults for the running user?
Choose 1 answer.

A. Anonymous Blocks
B. Apex Triggers
C. Web Service Callouts
D. Apex Classes

Question 39:
If a developer needs to skip to the next iteration of a loop, what loop control structure should be used?
Choose 1 answer.

A. skip;
B. end;
C. continue;
D. break;

Question 40:
A developer needs to do a quick one-time load of 100 custom object records into a development environment. The data is in a csv file and each record contains 5 fields. Which tool would you recommend to use to load the data?
Choose 1 answer.

A. Custom Object Import Wizard
B. Data API Tools
C. Data Loader
D. Data Import Wizard

Question 41:
In the opportunity record, the Salesforce Administrator needs to display the name of the parent account related to an account that is associated with the opportunity. How can this be accomplished?
Choose 1 answer.

A. Add a custom field with an account lookup
B. Create a custom field for the parent account name and use a workflow field update to update it with the parent account name
C. Create a cross object formula field to reference the parent account name
D. Create a custom field with a dependent lookup filter on account.

Question 42:
A company is performing a code review for a custom Salesforce application they have built to identify any security vulnerabilities before releasing it in production. Given the following code, what should be advised?
Choose 1 answer.

```
String dep = ApexPages.currentPage().getParameters().get('department');
if (dep != null) {
    String query = 'SELECT Id, Name from ' + dep + ' limit 10';
    // some code here
}
```

A. It is not advisable to use string queries. Refrain from using those.
B. Add more fields and expand limits [limit 10] on string query to refine search.
C. Compare the variable 'dep' against expected values instead of null
D. Use a variable instead of getting a parametric value on the URL.

Question 43:
A Salesforce Developer working for Cosmic Traders would like to create a custom Lightning App page in Lightning App Builder to meet a particular business requirement. Which of the following can be added to the Lightning page?
Choose 2 answers.

A. Standard components
B. Primary components
C. Object-specific actions
D. Global actions

Question 44:
How can a developer start and monitor debug logs via the Salesforce UI?
Choose 1 answer.

A. Setup > Profile > Choose Profile > Enable Debug Logs
B. Setup > User > Debug Logs > New
C. Setup > Company Information > Enable Debug Logs
D. Setup > Environments -> Logs > Debug Logs -> New

Question 45:
A Salesforce Administrator needs to get records with locations saved in geolocation or address fields as individual latitude and longitude values. Which SOQL statement accomplishes this goal?
Choose 1 answer.

A. SELECT Id, Name, Location__latitude__s, Location__longitude__s FROM CustomObject__c
B. SELECT Id, Name, Location__latitude__c, Location__longitude__c FROM CustomObject__c
C. SELECT Id, Name, Location__r.latitude__c, Location__r.longitude__c FROM CustomObject__c
D. SELECT Id, Name, Location__r.latitude, Location__r.longitude FROM CustomObject__c

Question 46:
Which are true regarding how to display data in a Visualforce page?
Choose 2 answers.

A. Object data can be inserted but not global data
B. Expression syntax is used to bind components to the data set available in the page controller
C. The <apex:fieldValue> component can be used to display individual fields from a record
D. Data context is provided to controllers by the id parameter of the page

Question 47:
A developer has created the custom controller below for a Visualforce page. Which of the following is the correct method of using a static query with a bind variable to prevent a SOQL injection attack? Choose 1 answer.

```
public class CustomContactController {
  public String name {
    get { return name;}
    set { name = value;}
  }

  private List<Contact> queryResult;
  public List<Contact> getQueryResult() {
    return queryResult;
  }

  public PageReference query() {
    String qryString = 'SELECT Id FROM Contact WHERE ' +
      '(IsDeleted = false and Name LIKE \'%' + name + '%\')';
    queryResult = Database.query(qryString);
    return null;
  }
}
```

A.
String queryName = '%' + name + '%';
queryResult = [SELECT Id FROM Contact WHERE (IsDeleted = false AND Name LIKE queryName)];

B.
queryResult = Database.query('SELECT Id FROM Contact WHERE ' + '(IsDeleted = false and Name LIKE \'%' + name + '%\')');

C.
String queryName = '%' + name + '%';
queryResult = [SELECT Id FROM Contact WHERE (IsDeleted = false AND Name LIKE :queryName)];

D.
queryResult = 'SELECT Id FROM Contact WHERE ' + '(IsDeleted = false and Name LIKE \'%' + name + '%\')';

Question 48:
Which of the following statements are true about trace flags?
Choose 2 answers.

A. Trace flag configuration is only available in the Salesforce UI setup
B. A trace flag includes a debug level, a start time, an end time, and a log type
C. A trace flag contains a specific debug level where a log category can have multiple log levels
D. Trace flags are assigned debug levels to activate debug logs for users and Apex classes and triggers

Question 49:
Which of the following statements are true when defining Apex classes?
Choose 2 answers.

A. It is optional to specify an access modifier in declaring inner class.
B. It is required to specify an access modifier in declaring top-level class.
C. A top-level class can have multiple levels of inner classes.
D. It is optional to specify an access modifier in declaring a top-level class.

Question 50:
A flow encountered an error in an org and sent an email notification to a Salesforce Administrator. The Salesforce Administrator would like to debug the failed flow interview in Flow Builder. However, a link to the flow interview was not included in the sent email. Which of the options below could be possible reasons?
Choose 2 answers.

A. The error was caused by an Action element in a screen flow.
B. The flow interview came from a platform event-triggered flow.
C. The flow belongs to a managed package and is not a template.
D. The status field of the flow is not set to 'Draft' or 'InvalidDraft'.

Question 51:
Given the following options, what data type should the developer use to store queried records via SOQL?
Choose 1 answer.

A. List
B. Group
C. Enum
D. Container

Question 52:
How can a dynamic SOQL query be created at runtime using input from an end user?
Choose 1 answer.

A. Use the Database.execute(string) with a query specified in the string
B. Use the SOQL.execute(string) with a query specified in the string
C. Use the Database.search(string) with a query specified in the string
D. Use the Database.query(string) with a query specified in the string

Question 53:
Given the code below, what will be the result?
Choose 1 answer.

```
Integer i = 0;
String str = '';

for (Integer x = 0; x < 10; x++) {
  str = 'sampleStr';
  i = x;
}

if (i > 9) {
  system.debug(str + ' A = ' + i);
} else if (i < 9) {
  system.debug(str + ' B = ' + i);
} else {
  system.debug(str + ' C = ' + i);
}
```

A. sampleStr A = 10
B. str B = 10
C. sampleStr C = 9
D. str B = 9

Question 54:
A developer has written an Apex Trigger. She tested it and the trigger is not functioning as expected. She now wants to debug the code. How can the developer accomplish this in the Developer Console?
Choose 1 answer.

A. Go to the Logs tab in Developer Console.
B. Go to the Anonymous Window in Developer Console.
C. Go to the Progress tab in Developer Console.
D. Go to the Run Tests in Developer Console.

Question 55:
Sam has completed a solution design and is ready to create the data model for a new application in Salesforce. There are a number of custom objects, each with a number of custom fields and relationships between the custom objects. What would you suggest to complete the task most efficiently?
Choose 1 answer.

A. Use the Schema Builder to create custom objects and fields, and then create relationships in Setup via Create->Objects
B. Use the Schema Builder to create custom objects, fields, and relationships
C. Create the Custom objects, fields, and relationships in Setup via Create->Objects and use the Schema Builder to verify that the data model was created correctly.
D. Use the Create Custom Field in Setup to create objects, fields, and relationships

Question 56:
What are valid use cases for using a controller extension in a Visualforce page?
Choose 2 answers.

A. To replace the standard controller entirely
B. To set any page to always run in system mode
C. To add a new action in the Visualforce page
D. To override the edit action of a standard controller

Question 57:
Which of the following should a Salesforce developer keep in mind about getter and setter methods in Visualforce?
Choose 3 answers.

A. Getter methods retrieve user input from the page markup and pass the input value to the controller.
B. Getter methods must always be named getVariable while setter methods must always be named setVariable.
C. While a getter method is always required to access values from a controller, it's not always necessary to include a setter method to pass values into a controller.
D. Any setter methods in a controller are automatically executed before any action methods.
E. Getter methods may include incrementing a variable, writing a log message, or adding a new record to the database.

Question 58:
A Salesforce developer needs to create a Visualforce custom controller for an object. What security implications and practices should the developer be aware of?
Choose 2 answers.

A. By default, Visualforce custom controllers run in system mode
B. By default, Visualforce custom controllers run with the logged-in user's security settings
C. To prevent unauthorized access, the 'with sharing' keywords should be used when declaring the class
D. To prevent unauthorized access, the 'without sharing' keywords should be used when declaring the class

Question 59:
Cosmic solutions has identified that sales reps being unaware of their upgrade prospects' open support cases causes them to lose sales. In response to this, a Salesforce developer has been tasked with creating a lightning component that will be placed on the opportunity record page. This component will display some key information about the opportunity's account, along with a table of open cases related to that account. The component's server-side controller must efficiently query the data to pass back to the component. Which query will provide the component with the appropriate data?
Choose 1 answer.

A. SELECT Name, AnnualRevenue, (SELECT CaseNumber, Status, Subject FROM Case__r WHERE IsClosed = FALSE) FROM Account WHERE Id = :accountId
B. SELECT Name, AnnualRevenue, (SELECT CaseNumber, Status, Subject FROM Cases__r WHERE IsClosed = FALSE) FROM Account WHERE Id = :accountId
C. SELECT Name, AnnualRevenue, (SELECT CaseNumber, Status, Subject FROM Case WHERE IsClosed = FALSE) FROM Account WHERE Id = :accountId
D. SELECT Name, AnnualRevenue, (SELECT CaseNumber, Status, Subject FROM Cases WHERE IsClosed = FALSE) FROM Account WHERE Id = :accountId

Question 60:
Which of the following methods in custom controllers allow the use of the @future annotation in custom controllers?
Choose 2 answers.

A. Getter methods
B. Setter methods
C. Methods containing DML statements
D. Methods containing web service callouts

SAMPLE EXAM II ANSWER KEY

Question 1 Answer:
A. Schema Builder

Schema Builder provides a dynamic environment for viewing and modifying all the objects and relationships in your app. You can view your existing schema and interactively add new custom objects, custom fields, and relationships, simply by dragging and dropping.

Question 2 Answer:
A. It is possible to have multiple extensions on a single Visualforce page, and extensions can be reused on different pages.
B. LeadExtA, LeadExtB, or LeadExtC cannot be used without the 'Lead' standard controller.
E. LeadExtA, LeadExtB, and LeadExtC are controller extensions used by the Visualforce page.

Multiple controller extensions can be defined for a single page through a comma-separated list. Overrides are defined by whichever methods are defined in the 'leftmost' extension, or, the extension that is first in the comma-separated list. In this case, it should be the LeadExtA.

Extensions are required to extend either a standard controller or a custom controller. In the above scenario, the 'Lead' standard controller would be required. Extensions can be reused on different Visualforce pages. Developers should plan ahead and use inheritance, either from a superclass or an interface, so to avoid too many constructors.

As with all controller methods, controller extension methods can be referenced with {! } notation in page markup, so the <apex:outputText> component will display its value.

Question 3 Answer:
D. Create valid test data for testing. Execute the methods to be tested and verify the expected results using assertions.

A unit test should:
(1) Set up all conditions for testing – Your unit tests should always create their own test data to execute against. That way, you can be confident that your tests are not dependent upon the state of a particular environment and will be repeatable even if they are executed in a different environment from which they were written.

(2) Call the method (or Trigger) being tested. – DML statements will invoke triggers.

(3) Verify that the results are correct. – A good way to tell if unit tests are properly verifying results is to look for liberal use of the System.assert() methods. If there are not any System.assert() method calls, then the tests are not verifying results properly.

Question 4 Answer:
B. A dynamic number of records can be rendered on the page
C. Pagination of records
E. Existing List View filters can be applied

Existing List View filters can be applied by using the {! listviewOptions } and {! filterId } variables. The standard "Recently Viewed Cases" list view would be appropriate for this scenario.
Rendering a dynamic number of records is accomplished by setting the {! PageSize } with an element that can set variables, such as an <apex:selectList>.
There are several options for pagination including Next, Previous, First, and Last actions.

Dynamic sorting is not available through Standard List Controllers. A custom controller would be required to implement this feature. The same applies to running calculations on fields before saving.

Question 5 Answer:
A. It is a best practice to have separate development and testing environments
C. At least 2 environments are required

Apex development can only be performed in a sandbox org. Hence, at least two orgs will be required, which are the production org and sandbox org.

Although at least two environments are required, it is best practice to have at least 3 environments – one for development, one for testing, and the production environment.

Question 6 Answer:
D. Order Required

In this case, the developer has used a switch statement to test an expression against several values. After winning a sales deal, when the value of the 'StageName' field on an opportunity is set to 'Closed Won' by a sales representative, the value of the 'Status__c' field on the opportunity is automatically updated to 'Order Required' once the code block for the 'when' value of 'Closed Won' is executed. The other 'when' values within the switch statement are ignored.

Question 7 Answer:
B. Ant Migration Tool

The Ant Migration Tool, which is a Java/Ant-based command-line utility used for moving metadata between a local directory and a Salesforce org, can be used to propagate destructive changes or delete components from a target org.

Change sets and unmanaged packages cannot be used to delete components. Data Loader is used to insert, update, delete, or export Salesforce records.

SALESFORCE CERTIFIED PLATFORM DEVELOPER I - RAPID CERTIFICATION EXAM PREP GUIDE

Question 8 Answer:
B. Package Development

In Package Development, every customization is managed as a single, separately-deployable unit and all changes are tracked in source control. Continuous integration and delivery is used in conjunction with version control to automate the promotion of functionality into higher environments. Both Org Development and Package Development deploy changes via deployment tools such as VSCode or the Salesforce CLI. Salesforce CLI (Command Line Interface) is a tool used in Org and Package Development but is not in itself a development model. Change Set Development also does not use source control and does not necessarily deploy functionality as self-enclosed packages.

Question 9 Answer:
C. Setter Method

Setter Method – The [set] method is used to pass values from the Visualforce page to the controller. Setter methods pass user-specified values from page markup to a controller. Any setter methods in a controller are automatically executed before any action methods.

Developer may create a method like this one:

```
public void setNum1(Integer Int1){
num1 = Int1;
}

public void setNum2(Integer Int2){
num2 = Int2;
}
```

in which Int1 and Int2 are the set values on the page, provided that a get method is also created for num1 and num2.

Question 10 Answer:
D. renderAs='pdf'

A developer can generate a downloadable, printable PDF file of a Visualforce page using the PDF rendering service. A Visualforce page rendered as a PDF file displays either in the browser or is downloaded, depending on the browser's settings. Specific behavior depends on the browser, version, and user settings, and is outside the control of Visualforce.

Question 11 Answer:
C. isExecuting

The isExecuting context variable returns true if any code inside the trigger context is executing. This means that a particular trigger can be tested whether it is executing or not with the help of this variable.

oldMap is a variable available only in update and delete triggers that contain a map of IDs to the old versions of the records processed by the trigger. The isUndelete and isUpdate trigger context variables return true after undelete and update operations respectively.

Question 12 Answer:
D. List<List<sObject>>

SOSL statements evaluate to a list of lists of sObjects. Therefore, to store the search results of a SOSL query, <List<List<sObject>>> can be used in Apex. Each list contains the search results for a particular sObject type. If no records are returned for a specified sObject type, the search results include an empty list for that sObject.

Question 13 Answer:
B. Double num = 1234.5;
C. Decimal num = 12345;

Primitive numeric data types form a hierarchy where lower types can be implicitly converted to higher types such as Integer -> Long -> Double -> Decimal. In the example statement above, an Integer can be assigned to a variable of Decimal data type without explicitly converting it to Decimal because Integer is a lower type compared to the Decimal type. Any number with decimal values can be assigned to a Double data type as long as the number is within the minimum and maximum limits of the Double data type.

A number with decimal values cannot be implicitly converted to Integer or Long types since Double and Decimal are higher types compared to Integer and Long.

Question 14 Answer:
D.
Boolean hasAssigned = getContact().Account?.isSet('Has_Primary_Contact__c ');

The safe navigation operator can be used for replacing explicit checks for null references and uses the syntax "?.", which is a question mark followed by a period. If the left-hand side of the operator evaluates to null, null is returned. Otherwise, the right-hand side, which can contain a method, variable, or property, is chained to the left-hand side of the operator and returned. In this case, the chained value is the 'isSet' method.

So, in the correct answer above, the resulting value that is returned to the 'hasAssigned' variable will be expressed as getContact().Account.isSet('Has_Primary_Contact__c ') if the contact is related to an account.

The other options contain invalid syntax or return values.

Question 15 Answer:
C. Page.existingPageName;
D. PageReference pageRef = new PageReference('URL');

Page.existingPageName, where 'existingPageName' represents the name of the Visualforce page, can be used to reference a PageReference instance of a Visualforce page.

A PageReference of a Visualforce page can also be instantiated by specifying its URL. For example: PageReference pageRef = new PageReference('URL');

In addition, a PageReference for the current page can be instantiated by using the ApexPages.currentPage() method. For example: PageReference pageRef = ApexPages.currentPage();.

Question 16 Answer:
A. Apex custom controllers
B. Visualforce Controllers

The control layer includes business logic either declarative (like workflow and escalation rules) or programmatic (like Visualforce controllers or Apex classes). The controller is responsible for responding to the user input and perform interactions on the data model objects. The controller receives the input, it validates the input and then performs the business operation that modifies the state of the data model.

Question 17 Answer:
B. Define a Unique External ID field on the Account object and populate it with unique record identifiers from the external system.
C. Add unique record identifiers from the account records in the external system to the .csv file and use it to insert the new records.

A Unique External ID field defined on a parent object in Salesforce, such as the Account object, can be used to import and relate associated child records, such as contacts. The External ID field can be used to identify and relate the parent account records to the child contacts during the import process. The values of the field can be added to the .csv file that is used for inserting the new related contact records. Creating an Apex trigger is not necessary to relate the records. Developing a custom integration in the external system to obtain Salesforce record IDs would require more effort and resources, so it is not the recommended solution.

Question 18 Answer:
C. Governor limits ensure that the amount of CPU time is monitored and limited per customer over a defined time period to ensure that performance in one org is not impacted by another
D. Restrictions are enforced on code that can be deployed into a production environment

Although many customers share the same instance, it is not possible for one customer query to return data from another customer. Each row in the table that stores application data includes identifying fields, such as the organization that owns the row (OrgID).

The total API requests (calls) per 24-hour period is limited for an org. Governor limits monitor and limit various factors such as CPU time and DML statements to ensure that one org does not impact another. Code cannot be deployed into production unless test code coverage is achieved.

Question 19 Answer:
A. Archive
C. Style Sheet
D. JavaScript File

Archives, Images, Style Sheets and JavaScript files are content that can be uploaded as static resources and referenced in Visualforce pages using the $Resource global variable.

Although Salesforce does not prevent users from uploading actual Apex class (*.cls) or trigger (*.tgr) files into Static Resources, these files cannot be referenced in Visualforce pages this way. An Apex class, for example, is referenced through the controller or extensions attribute defined on a Visualforce page.

Question 20 Answer:
B. <apex:iframe>

The <apex:iframe> component is used to create an inline frame within a Visualforce page. It can be used to load external websites and/or allow viewing certain information on the page while other information is scrolled or replaced.

The <apex:include> component is used to load another Visualforce page in a current Visualforce page. The <apex:getsite> or <apex:output> tags do not exist.

Question 21 Answer:
B. 1st, 2nd, 3rd, & 4th

The execution unit begins on line 1 with EXECUTION_STARTED, ends on line 4 with EXECUTION_FINISHED, and contains everything that occurred within the transaction, including the CODE UNIT on lines 2 and 3.

Question 22 Answer:
B. Static methods
D. Setter methods

DML statements can't be used in getter or constructor methods, but they can be used in setter and static methods.

Question 23 Answer:
B. $IFrameResource.<resource_name>
Static resources that are downloaded from an untrusted third-party source can be isolated using an iframe on a Visualforce page. This adds an extra layer of security to the page and helps protect the assets. To reference a static HTML file on a separate domain, $IFrameResource.<resource_name> can be used as a merge field, where 'resource_name' is the name of the static resource.

Question 24 Answer:
C. The [Rerun Failed Tests] option reruns only the failed tests from the test run that are highlighted in the Tests tab.
D. If the test run includes more than one test class, the Developer Console always runs tests asynchronously in the background.
E. An Overall Code Coverage pane is available that displays the percentage of code coverage for each class in org.

The Suite Manager is used to create or delete test suites or edit which classes a particular test suite contains. A test suite is a collection of Apex test classes that are run together. The New Suite option is used to group test classes that are run together. It cannot be used to create a test class. The Developer Console runs tests asynchronously by default. Tests are run synchronously only when there is only one test class being run and the [Always Run Asynchronously] option is not checked. If multiple test classes are run, the test will always be run asynchronously whether or not the [Always Run Asynchronously] option is checked.

Question 25 Answer:
B. Flow
D. Process Builder

Custom Notifications can be created to push notification messages to Salesforce users on desktop and mobile. Currently, Custom Notifications can be pushed from Process Builder, Flow, and the REST API. Workflow Rules and Approval Processes do not currently support sending Custom Notifications.

Question 26 Answer:
C. Create a platform event-triggered flow and specify the platform event.
D. Use the $Record global variable to access field values in the event message.

A platform event-triggered flow created in Flow Builder can subscribe to a specific platform event. When a platform event message is published, it invokes the flow, which can perform the necessary record updates based on the event message data available in the $Record global variable.

CometD is used to allow external applications to subscribe to platform events. Although an Apex trigger can also be used to subscribe to the platform event and meet the requirement, using a declarative solution is recommended by Salesforce.

SALESFORCE CERTIFIED PLATFORM DEVELOPER I - RAPID CERTIFICATION EXAM PREP GUIDE

Question 27 Answer:
A. try { *code here* } catch (Exception e) { *code here* } finally { *code here* }

In a try-catch-finally statement, the main business logic is executed in the try block. If an error occurs within the try block, it will be caught and handled by the catch block. Then, whether or not an exception was caught, code in the finally block will always be executed as the last phase in the control flow. Finally statements can be used to perform cleanup code such as for freeing up resources.

Question 28 Answer:
A. Total number of records retrieved by SOQL queries
B. CPU time per transaction
C. Time executing a SOQL query

The runtime engine enforces limits of how long a SOQL query can run, how many records can be returned in a query and the maximum amount of CPU time a transaction can take. The maximum number of records that can be stored in an object is dependent on the storage available and is not subject to a governor limit.

Unlike SOQL queries, there is no maximum execution time for DML statements. There is, however, a limit for the total number of DML statements that can be executed in an Apex transaction.

Question 29 Answer:
A. It will rollback all changes made up to the error.
D. An exception will be thrown.

One transaction may contain different operations and processes including but not limited to DML calls made by different classes, controllers, triggers, flows and workflow rules. If, at any point in the transaction the governor limit is exceeded, all changes are rolled back up to the error, and a Limit Exception is thrown, exiting the entire execution process.

So, whichever component or operation in the process that caused it to reach the governor limit is not significant. No changes will be committed to the database. In addition, governor limits throw exceptions which cannot be handled (try catch blocks).

Question 30 Answer:
A. Methods that are annotated with @future identify methods that are executed asynchronously.
D. Methods annotated with @future can only return a void type.

The future annotation is used to identify methods that are executed asynchronously, and only return a void type. When you specify the future, the method executes when Salesforce has available resources.

Question 31 Answer:
C. Enable 'Launch Flow on Rejection' for the Next Best Action component in Lightning App Builder
D. Build a single flow to perform an action that is used when a recommendation is accepted or rejected

A recommendation can only invoke one and the same flow when it is either accepted or rejected by the user. By default, a recommendation only launches the flow when it is accepted. To also launch the flow when it is rejected, a Decision element is added to the flow that specifically uses an "isRecommendationAccepted" boolean variable for determining whether the recommendation that launched it was approved or rejected, and then perform the necessary logic in the flow accordingly. Also, the 'Launch Flow on Rejection' settings for the Next Best Action component must be enabled in Lightning App Builder.

Question 32 Answer:
A. The related record can have a different owner than the parent record.
B. The lookup field does not need to be a required field on the page layout.

When using master-detail relationships, the child record inherits the record owner of the parent record. On the other hand, in lookup relationships, the child record can have a different owner.

Lookup relationship fields do not need to be marked as required on the page layout. Roll-up summary fields can only be added to the parent object in a master-detail relationship. Lookup relationships do not support creating roll-up summary fields.

In a lookup relationship, if a parent record is deleted, the child records are only deleted when the option to 'Delete this record also' is selected, which is only available if a custom object contains the lookup relationship.

Question 33 Answer:
A. Formula field
B. Workflow Field Update
D. Apex Class

Below is a list of some of the components that when a field is referenced, the reference should be deleted or updated first before the field can be deleted: Apex Class, Apex Trigger, Visualforce Page, Visualforce Component, Workflow Rule, Field Update, Criteria-Based Sharing Rule, Flow, Jobs, etc.

Question 34 Answer:
D. Create a flow that sends a survey invitation to the contact automatically when the value of the custom field changes.

Flow Builder can be used to create a flow that executes an action type called 'Send Survey Invitation'. It can automatically email survey invitations to leads, contacts, or users. In this case, the flow can be triggered automatically when the value of the custom field changes.

Using a native action in a flow is better than relying on an outbound message and a third-party system. It is also better to meet this requirement declaratively instead of using an Apex trigger. Although a process created using Process Builder may also send a survey after a record change, moving forward, flow is the recommended declarative automation solution by Salesforce as it has better performance.

Question 35 Answer:
A. !a.Opportunities.isEmpty()
D. opps.addAll(a.Opportunities);

To determine if a SOQL result is empty or not, the method isEmpty() can be used. The method isNotEmpty() is not a valid method in Apex. To add a list to a List collection, the addAll() method is used. The add() method is used for adding a single element to a List collection.

The result of a subquery can be retrieved for each record of the returned list by using the child relationship name, which the same name that is used in the subquery FROM clause. For standard objects, that would be the standard plural form of the sObject name (e.g. Contacts, Leads, etc.). For custom objects, the __r suffix, which indicates a custom relationship, is needed (e.g. Appointments__r).

Question 36 Answer:
A. Account acc = new Account();

In the correct answer, a new Account object is initialized to the 'acc' variable. However, other options are incorrectly assigned to its variable. The proper way should be:

String a = 'sampleString';
Map<Id, Account> mapAcc = new Map<Id, Account>([SELECT Id, Name FROM Account]);
List<Contact> conList = [SELECT Id FROM Contact];

Question 37 Answer:
D. SELECT Account.Name, Account.BillingState FROM Contact WHERE Account.BillingState=\'Arizona\' LIMIT 50
E. SELECT Name, (SELECT LastName, FirstName FROM Contacts) FROM Account WHERE BillingState=\'Arizona\' LIMIT 50

A relationship query is a query on multiple related standard or custom objects. To create a join in SOQL, a relationship between the objects is required. Using a relationship query, it is possible to traverse parent-to-child and child-to-parent relationships between objects to filter and return results. For example, a SOQL query that returns data from the Account object can also retrieve the first and last name of each contact associated with each account returned by the query.

Dot notation is used to reference fields from parent objects, while a nested SELECT statement is used to query child records. Dot notation can\'t be used to query fields on child records, and nested SELECT statements can\'t be used to retrieve parent data. Standard child relationship names use the plural form of the child object as the relationship name, so from an Account object, the relationship to Contact records is named Contacts.

Question 38 Answer:
A. Anonymous Blocks

The [with sharing] keyword allows us to specify that the sharing rules for the current user be taken into account for a class. The developer has to explicitly set this keyword for the class because the Apex code runs in the system context. In the system context, the Apex code has access to all objects and fields. Object permissions, field-level security, and sharing rules are not applied for the current user. This is to ensure that the code will not fail to run because of hidden fields or objects for a user. The only exception to this rule is the Apex code that is executed with the executeAnonymous call. executeAnonymous always executes using the permissions of the current user.

Question 39 Answer:
C. continue;

The "continue" keyword is used to skip the current iteration of a loop and proceed to the next one.

The "break" keyword is used to exit the entire loop. The "end" and "skip" are invalid keywords.

Question 40 Answer:
D. Data Import Wizard

The data import wizard will allow importing of selected standard objects and all custom objects. The key decision points in this description: \'one-time\' means you don\'t need to save the import mappings for repeated use, as Data Loader and more comprehensive tools can do; 100 records with 5 fields is low volume; each \'custom object\' means that Data Import Wizard is capable of importing these records, unlike records for some of the unsupported standard objects.

Question 41 Answer:
C. Create a cross object formula field to reference the parent account name

A cross-object formula field can be created on the Opportunity object to display the parent account. Cross-object formula fields can reference fields up to 10 levels away.

Creating a custom field on the Account object to store the parent account is not necessary as the standard Parent Account field is available for this use case. Using a workflow rule to associate the parent account to an opportunity is not necessary because of the formula field.

Question 42 Answer:
C. Compare the variable 'dep' against expected values instead of null

Using the defined Departments, define exact conditions when validating the variable 'dep' and avoid using null. A good solution is an "allowlist", or a list of known good values that the user input should conform to.

To prevent SOQL injection, add in allowlisting by verifying that the value of the [department] URL parameter conforms to one of the expected values, e.g. FINANCE, ENGINEERING, SECURITY, HEALTH.

Question 43 Answer:
A. Standard components
D. Global actions

Standard, custom, and third-party components can be added to the Lightning page. Global actions can be added via the Actions attribute of the Lightning App page properties, which is only possible for this Lightning page type. The other Lightning page types derive their actions from the object and global page layouts.

There are only standard, custom, and third-party Lightning components. There are no "primary" components. Object-specific actions are added to the page layout of an object.

Question 44 Answer:
D. Setup > Environments -> Logs > Debug Logs -> New

From Setup, Debug Logs can be found within Environments -> Logs.

Select the entity to trace, the time period during which you want to collect logs, and a debug level.

Question 45 Answer:
A. SELECT Id, Name, Location__latitude__s, Location__longitude__s FROM CustomObject__c

Records with locations saved in geolocation or address fields as individual latitude and longitude values can be retrieved by appending '__latitude__s' or '__longitude__s' to the field name, instead of the usual '__c'.

Question 46 Answer:
B. Expression syntax is used to bind components to the data set available in the page controller
D. Data context is provided to controllers by the id parameter of the page

Both object (sObjects) and global (profiles, users, company, locale, etc.) data can be inserted using the expression syntax. The <apex:outputField> component can be used to display individual fields from a record.

Question 47 Answer:
C.
String queryName = '%' + name + '%';
queryResult = [SELECT Id FROM Contact WHERE (IsDeleted = false AND Name LIKE :queryName)];

In order to prevent a SOQL injection attack, instead of using a dynamic SOQL query, static query and bind variable can be used, such as below.

String queryName = '%' + name + '%';
List<Contact> queryResult = [SELECT Id FROM Contact WHERE (IsDeleted = false AND Name LIKE :queryName)];
When binding variables in a static query, a colon is added before the variable. Dynamic queries require the Database query method.

Question 48 Answer:
B. A trace flag includes a debug level, a start time, an end time, and a log type
D. Trace flags are assigned debug levels to activate debug logs for users and Apex classes and triggers

A debug level is a set of log levels for debug log categories (Database, Workflow, Validation, etc.) and can be reused across trace flags. Each trace flag can only be assigned to one debug level. One debug level covers multiple categories where each category is assigned one specific log level. Trace flags and debug levels can be configured in the Developer Console and Salesforce UI.

Question 49 Answer:
A. It is optional to specify an access modifier in declaring inner class.
B. It is required to specify an access modifier in declaring top-level class.

It is mandatory to specify one of the access modifiers when declaring a top-level class, while it is not mandatory to specify an access modifier when declaring inner classes. You must use one of the access modifiers (such as public or global) in the declaration of a top-level class. The private access modifier declares that the class is only known locally. The default access for inner classes is private. If the access modifier is not specified for an inner class, it is considered private. Inner classes can only be one level deep.

Question 50 Answer:
B. The flow interview came from a platform event-triggered flow.
C. The flow belongs to a managed package and is not a template.

When a screen flow, record-triggered flow, scheduled-triggered flow, or autolaunched flow with no trigger launches and encounters an error, the failed flow interview is saved in the org. The notification email that contains details of the error includes a link that allows the recipient to access the saved flow interview in Flow Builder and debug the flow more efficiently.

However, a failed flow interview is not saved in all the instances. For example, the flow interview is not saved if the error came from a platform event-triggered flow, the flow is not active, the flow came from a managed package and is not a template, the error was thrown as a result of an Apex test method, and more. If the flow interview was not saved, then the notification email does not include a link.

A failed flow interview of a screen flow is saved if it is active, for example, regardless of the element that threw an exception. If the status metadata field of a flow is 'Draft' or 'InvalidDraft', then its failed flow interviews are not saved.

Question 51 Answer:
A. List

A list is an ordered collection of elements that are distinguished by their indices. List should be used for storing queried records via SOQL. A map can also be used.

Group and Container are invalid data types. An Enum data type is used to store a value from a finite set of identifiers that are specified.

Question 52 Answer:
D. Use the Database.query(string) with a query specified in the string

The Database.query(string) method can be used to return a single or list of sObjects.

Question 53 Answer:
C. sampleStr C = 9

The for loop will iterate the code block until the value of x = 9. The value of x, which is 9, will be assigned to variable [i]. So variable [int] will satisfy the third condition. Expected output will be: sampleStr C = 9

Question 54 Answer:
A. Go to the Logs tab in Developer Console.

The logs tab in the developer console is used to open and inspect debug logs. The debug logs includes database events, Apex processing, workflow, and validation logic.

Question 55 Answer:
B. Use the Schema Builder to create custom objects, fields, and relationships

Schema Builder can be used to efficiently create a number of objects, fields, and relationships in less time than creating the objects
in Setup.

Question 56 Answer:
C. To add a new action in the Visualforce page
D. To override the edit action of a standard controller

A controller extension is an Apex class that is used to extend the functionality of a standard or custom controller. It enables a page to override actions, such as edit, view, save, or delete. It can also add new actions and is not used as a replacement of the standard or custom controller it leverages on. Though a controller extension typically executes in system mode, it will execute in user mode when used as an extension of a standard controller.

Question 57 Answer:
B. Getter methods must always be named getVariable while setter methods must always be named setVariable.
C. While a getter method is always required to access values from a controller, it's not always necessary to include a setter method to pass values into a controller.
D. Any setter methods in a controller are automatically executed before any action methods.

Setter methods pass user input values from a form, for example, on a Visualforce page to pass it to the controller. Hence, setter methods are automatically executed before any action method is called. Setter methods are not always required in order to pass values to the controller such as when a Visualforce inputField component is bound to a record field in the controller.

Getter methods are designed to retrieve values only and should not include record or value changes such as incrementing a member variable or updating a field value on a record.

Question 58 Answer:
A. By default, Visualforce custom controllers run in system mode
C. To prevent unauthorized access, the 'with sharing' keywords should be used when declaring the class

Unlike standard controllers, custom controllers run in system mode by default, unless the 'with sharing' keywords are specified.

Question 59 Answer:
D. SELECT Name, AnnualRevenue, (SELECT CaseNumber, Status, Subject FROM Cases WHERE IsClosed = FALSE) FROM Account WHERE Id = :accountId

A subquery (a parent-to-child relationship query) is used to retrieve a list of related child records for each retrieved parent record and is written inside parentheses in the SELECT clause. A subquery's FROM clause uses the child relationship name of the lookup relationship on the child. For standard objects, this is generally the plural form of the object ('Cases' in this example).
Only custom objects append __r to the end of the child relationship name. The child relationship name can be found on the lookup field setup page in the object manager and on the org's WSDL file.

Question 60 Answer:
C. Methods containing DML statements
D. Methods containing web service callouts

Getter, setter, and constructor methods in custom controllers can't be annotated with @future since the processing of a page depends on these methods immediately returning or processing data. Methods containing DML statements or web service callouts can use the @future annotation.

ABOUT THE AUTHOR

BookWorm Channel provides accelerated learning series on popular topics.

Our goal is to provide bite-size information for beginners to learn more about a particular topic. We hope you enjoyed this content.

You can learn more about our upcoming books by visiting https://bookwormchannel.com.